Trustworthy AI

Trustworthy AI

*A Business Guide
for Navigating Trust and
Ethics in AI*

Beena Ammanath

WILEY

For general information on our other products and services or for technical
support, please contact our Customer Care Department within the United States at
(800) 762-2974, outside the United States at (317) 572-3993 or fax (317) 572-4002.

Wiley also publishes its books in a variety of electronic formats. Some content that
appears in print may not be available in electronic formats. For more information
about Wiley products, visit our web site at www.wiley.com.

Library of Congress Cataloging-in-Publication Data is Available:

ISBN: 9781119867920 (Hardback)
ISBN: 9781119867968 (ePdf)
ISBN: 9781119867951 (epub)

Cover Design: Wiley
Cover Image: Sunrise © titoOnz/Getty Images

SKY10032742_012622

Contents

Foreword

There are two kinds of organizations. Those that are fueled by artificial intelligence and those that will become fueled by AI. Eventually, all organizations public and private will be AI organizations. It is a twenty-first-century fact that efficiency, agility, competitiveness, and growth hinge on the successful use of AI. This is to the good, and the value is measured in trillions of dollars.

The potential, however, comes with a caveat. We cannot create world-changing solutions and use AI for all the beneficial purposes we can imagine unless this technology rests on a firm ethical foundation. What we do today to align AI function and use with human values sets the trajectory for this transformative technology for decades to come.

I have had wonderful opportunities to speak with government and business leaders from countries around the world. Questions about AI ethics and trust are being debated in boardrooms, business halls, legislative chambers, and the public square. What I've learned is that, on the one hand, there is a growing awareness of how ethics and trust affect the use of AI. On the other hand, this awareness is causing some wariness about whether AI should be used at all. This speaks to valid concern about the technical function and social impact of AI, but it also reveals a more fundamental need on the part of organizations deploying AI.

People want to trust AI, if only they could.

The good news is we can get there, and it will take important decisions and actions to set not just individual businesses but the entire world on the path to trustworthy AI.

More and more, leaders are realizing that we, as a global population, must act purposefully on AI ethics – and we must do so now. If we do, we can minimize the risks, maximize trust in the technology, and build toward the brightest future AI can facilitate.

Some might speculate that prioritizing ethics and trust could impede innovation at the moment when the power of AI is finally brought to fruition. I submit that the reverse is true. The most powerful and useful AI innovations are those that align with our ethics and values. What we do not trust, we will not use. We need to be able to trust cognitive tools to move forward with AI.

While the imperative is clear, the tactics and knowledge to address trust are somewhat less so. What ethics are relevant for AI use? What does it mean to trust a machine intelligence? Where are the hurdles, the pitfalls, and the great opportunities to build ethics into novel AI? The chorus of voices asking these questions and others like them is growing louder, and the refrain is the same: How do we get to a place where our AI tools are simultaneously powerful, valuable, and trustworthy?

For better or worse, there is not just one answer to that question. There are many possible answers. Every organization operates within a society, and communities, nations, and regions can have very different views and laws on morality, ethics, and standards for technology application. What is considered trustworthy in one place may not hold in another. The priority ethics in one industry may be secondary or tertiary matters in a different field. No two businesses are the same and so no two frameworks for AI ethics and trust will be identical.

Fortunately, however, we do not need to determine universal rules for trustworthy AI. What we do need is a clear and precise framework that lays out key questions and priorities, defines essential terms and concepts, sets waypoints and guideposts throughout the AI lifecycle, and orients the business strategy and the workforce toward supporting ethical AI.

This book is an asset for your efforts. Its author, Beena Ammanath, is a consummate expert on AI. An AI optimist, the lessons and insights she shares are born of her rich experience as a technologist and an executive working across numerous industries. In this book, Beena helps you cut through the noise and discover the knowledge and practical steps your organization needs for a trustworthy future with AI.

In the pages that follow, you will discover the many dimensions of AI ethics and trust, the questions they prompt, the priorities for the organization, and some of the best practices that contribute to trustworthy AI governance. One lesson that permeates this thoughtful investigation of trust is that enterprise leaders should resist the clarion call of "everyone uses AI, so must you." Fools rush in. Instead, AI application requires a close consideration of trust, with questions focused not just on whether the organization can use AI but whether it should, and if it does, how it can do so ethically.

As you read this book, consider how the lessons and insights can help your enterprise develop a plan for using AI. Think through goals, use cases, application, management, training, and policies and how the dimensions of trust influence and are influenced by these qualities. This book helps you conceive of a strong ethical foundation for AI and identify the plans and processes that engender confidence and trust in these powerful tools.

The capabilities and application of intelligent machines are evolving fast – even faster than most might realize. To capture the most benefit and mitigate the most challenges, we must take up the banner of trustworthy AI and carry it with us as we charge ahead into this bold new era with AI.

Kay Firth-Butterfield
Head of Artificial Intelligence and Machine Learning
World Economic Forum

Preface

There are clear turning points in human history, and we are in the midst of one. Artificial intelligence is changing the world before our eyes at a breathtaking pace. There is no segment of society nor slice of the market that will go untouched by AI, and this transformation has the potential to deliver the most positive impact of any technology we have yet devised. This is cause for optimism and excitement. The era of AI has arrived.

Today, we can predict jet engine failure to improve safety and prevent disruption. In medicine, we can detect diseases earlier and increase chances of patient recovery. Autonomous transportation is evolving across land, sea, air, and outer space. And every aspect of doing business is receiving new valuable, powerful solutions. Faster customer service, real-time planning adjustments, supply chain efficiency, even AI innovation itself – all have radically changed and improved with the cognitive tools now deployed at scale.

There has arguably never been a more exciting time in AI. Alongside the arrival of so much promise and potential, however, the attention placed on AI ethics has been relatively slight. What passes for public scrutiny is too often just seductive, click-bait headlines that fret over AI bias and point to a discrete use case. There's a lot of noise on AI ethics and trust, and it does not move us closer to clarity or consensus on how we keep trust in AI commensurate with its power.

Anyone who has worked in an enterprise understands the challenges inherent in integrating new technology. The tech implementation, training, equipment investments, process adjustments – seizing value with technology is no simple matter. How much more challenging then is it to simultaneously drive toward nebulous concepts around ethics and trust?

Yet, the challenge notwithstanding, enterprises do need to contend with these matters. Fortunately, there is every cause for optimism. We are not necessarily late in addressing trust and ethics in AI, but it is time for the organizations to get moving. That recognition was the catalyst for this book.

This is not the first time humanity has stood at the doorstep of innovation and been confronted with ethical unknowns. We should have confidence that we can devise methods for aligning technology, ethics, and our need for trust in the tools we use. The solutions are waiting for us to find them.

But there will never be just one solution, no one-size-fits-all answer to the question of trustworthy AI. From an organizational perspective, irrespective of whether you are developing AI or just using AI, every company has to identify what trustworthy AI means for the enterprise and then design, develop, and deploy to that vision.

When we consider all that AI can do (and will be able to do), it can be hard to temper our enthusiasm. When we think about how poor AI ethics could lead to bad outcomes, it can be difficult to see beyond our concerns. The path forward with AI is between these extremes – working toward the greatest benefit AI can enable while taking great care to ensure the tools we use reflect human values.

One shortcoming of how AI ethics are frequently debated is that it is seldom pertinent to the priorities of business leaders. We have all read a lot about racist chatbots and highly speculative fears about an imagined general AI. In place of this, we need a rich discussion on AI trust as it relates to business decision making and complex enterprise functions. The AI models used in businesses are far more varied than what is commonly discussed, and there are numerous stakeholders across business units, each of whom have different needs, goals, and concerns around AI.

So that we are not talking in the abstract, let's anchor our reading journey on a company that performs high-precision manufacturing – this is an imaginary company that exists only in the pages of this book, of course. The enterprise, called BAM Inc., is headquartered in the United States, runs manufacturing plants in three regions and six countries, and does about $4 billion in business annually. Like leaders in large companies in the real world, the executives at BAM Inc. get value from AI but also face uncertainties around trustworthy AI.

Each business unit aspires to greater productivity and success, and as AI tools are deployed, the problems they create require the executive leadership to make decisions on how to prevent issues before they occur and correct them if they do. By looking through the lenses of business leaders, we can probe the challenging nuances that every organization encounters during its maturation into an AI-fueled enterprise.

In the investigation of trust and ethics in the following chapters, we use BAM Inc. as a laboratory for exploring the challenges with trustworthy AI in the business environment. As we follow the company's AI saga, remember that the issues the business faces are arising in enterprises around the world. There are all-too-real boardroom conversations where leadership is facing an AI challenge but may lack the tools to find solutions.

The solutions are waiting to be discovered, and this book is a companion in the journey to finding them. Whether you are an executive, technologist, ethicist, engineer, user, or indeed anyone who touches the AI lifecycle, the ensuing chapters can equip you with the perspective, questions, and next steps for cultivating your future with trustworthy AI.

Acknowledgments

This book is the product of decades of professional experience, research, and AI application in a diverse set of industries, and by virtue of that, there are many people to whom I owe gratitude and acknowledgment for their valuable insights and support.

First, I thank Wiley for their readiness to publish this important work and their dedication to seeing it come to fruition.

I also offer my sincere thanks and appreciation to my colleagues, Nitin Mittal, Irfan Saif, Kwasi Mitchell, Dave Couture, Matt David, Costi Perricos, Kate Schmidt, Anuleka Ellan Saroja, David Thogmartin, Jesse Goldhammer, David Thomas, Sanghamitra Pati, Catherine Bannister, Masaya Mori, Gregory Abisror, and Michael Frankel.

I owe great thanks to the insights and discussions with colleagues and friends over the past several years – Lovleen Joshi, Archie Deskus, Dr. Abhay Chopada, Jana Eggers, Prajesh Kumar,

Dr. Sara Terheggen, Jim Greene, Colin Parris, Dr. Amy Fleischer, Vince Campisi, Rachel Trombetta, Justin Hienz, Tony Thomas, Deepa Naik, Tarun Rishi, Marcia Morales-Jaffe, Mike Dulworth, and Jude Schramm – who have helped shape my thinking on the myriad dimensions of technology.

This book and all of my life's work would not have been possible without the love and support of my parents, Kamalam and Kumar, my husband, Nikhil, and my sons, Neil and Sean. It is my hope that *Trustworthy AI* helps make this world a better place with all the benefits of AI and without many of the negative impacts. This is for my children – and yours, too.

Finally, thank you, reader, for taking this opportunity to explore trustworthy AI and seek ways to contribute to the ethical development of this powerful technology. We all share the responsibility to create and use AI for the greatest global benefit. Thank you for joining this important journey to a trustworthy future.

We can only see a short distance ahead,

but we can see plenty there that needs

to be done.

– Alan Turing

Introduction

The most significant factor that will impact our future with artificial intelligence is trust.

Our human society depends on trust – trust in one another, in our economic and governmental systems, and in the products and services we purchase and use. Without trust, we are plagued with uncertainty, suspicion, reticence, and even fear. Trust can be fragile, and once broken, nearly impossible to repair. And all the while, trust receives only passing notice as a vital part of our lives. We take it for granted and presume it is present, until it isn't.

This vital and uniquely human need to trust is today colliding with the powerful forces of technology innovation. For decades, AI has existed primarily in research labs, developed for novel experiments that incrementally move the field forward. This has changed. Advancing at a near exponential clip, AI tools are being developed and deployed in huge numbers. These technologies touch nearly every part of our connected lives.

We are commonly aware of the AI behind self-driving cars and chatbots that mimic human speech, but AI is much more pervasive. It fuels machine automation and predictive analysis across a range of functions. It powers back office operations and customer-facing communication. It leads to new products and services, new business models, and truly new ways of working and living. In short, the age of AI has arrived, and every citizen and organization must contend with what that means for our trust in the tools we use.

It is a question not just of what can be done with AI but how it should be done—or whether it should be done at all. Fundamentally, because AI has been developed to this level of maturity, we must now grapple with some of the more philosophical considerations around AI.

What does it mean for AI use to be ethical? How do we know if we can trust the AI tools we use? How do we know if we should?

It may be simultaneously intimidating and motivating that these questions, for the most part, have not been answered. Indeed, it is the absence of answers that is driving increasing focus among data scientists, business leaders, and government authorities alike on how we ensure this new era with AI is one we can trust and one we want.

History will record the early twenty-first century as a watershed moment in human civilization. Few inventions even come close to the potential in AI, though there are standout examples, such as the printing press, the internal combustion engine, and the CPU. AI is already yielding social and economic changes that are on par with (if not exceeding) the transformative impact of those innovations. It is impossible to overstate just how much AI is changing everything, and for that reason, we are obligated to think through the ethics of how these tools should be developed and used.

There is no corpus of literature and scholarship that defines ethics and trust in AI to a granular degree. There is no checklist that, if satisfied, yields trustworthy AI. We are not there yet. On the road to universal agreement on the qualities of ethical AI that can be trusted, those using AI have an important role to play. A data science background is not a prerequisite for participating in this journey. To the contrary, the rules, leading practices, considerations, and philosophies that can support the next decades with AI, as it fully matures into ever more powerful technologies, require the input of people from all fields and all walks of life.

Most simply, if an organization is using AI, everyone in that organization is already participating in shaping the AI era. And given that, there is a moral (if not strategic) imperative to equip people with the knowledge, processes, and teamwork they need to contribute meaningfully and responsibly to how the use of AI continues to unfold. Such is the purpose of this book.

The effort and attention required to ensure AI is trustworthy is significant, even daunting, but this is not the first time humanity has stood at the doorstep of technological revolution. History has lessons for us. Take the birth and mass adoption of personal automobiles. When gas-powered cars were first unveiled and public adoption grew fast, there were few of the rules, technologies, and standards that we have today.

When the first Model Ts rolled out of the factory, there were no speed limits or automated lights at intersections. There were no standard signs to guide traffic. Pedestrians had to learn to watch out for the nearly one-ton machines rattling down the road. Drivers had to learn how to safely operate the car. Legislators had to pass new laws governing the use of personal cars, and courts were pressed to hear cases where there was no precedent. Indeed, the consumer car became commonplace and because of that, a sociotechnical system evolved around it to govern how the world used this transformative technology.

To continue the analogy, AI is rolling out of the factory *en masse*, and we have few speed limits or seatbelts. These tools are powerful, but their power is comparatively meager relative to what is coming, which points to our current challenge. We must dedicate our efforts to developing the commensurate traffic lights, speed limits, and consumer regulations that can nurture a sociotechnical system that guides AI to its greatest, most trustworthy potential. How?

We can conceive of this task along three streams: research, application, and trust and ethics. Research is the province of data science and AI engineering. Visionaries and innovators can be found not just in academic labs but increasingly in private enterprise, where they push the envelope of AI capabilities. This stream has characterized much of the history of AI to date.

For several decades and accelerating, we have seen AI application in growing volume. This is more than the automation of repetitive tasks. AI can find patterns in vast datasets, it can accurately predict real-world conditions before they arrive, and it can engage with humans across all aspects of their lives. It is impacting every industry. Innovation is the byword of the day, and we are right to be excited. This is a fascinating time to be alive, to see such a technology and its impact become manifest.

The potential raises what is the increasingly important third stream – determining how to use this technology in an ethical way such that we can trust it. There is a growing consensus throughout the AI community that we must meet this challenge and do so now, when modern AI is in its relative infancy. That task falls on every organization using AI and ultimately, the onus for action falls initially on the leaders of these organizations. The sociotechnical system that will dictate how AI is used for years to come is being built today by enterprise leaders, regardless of whether they realize it.

Navigating the Innovation Curve

Solving for trust in AI is not just a virtuous endeavor that is now necessary. In business, it has a real impact on the bottom line, as well as on how customers view and engage with the organization. The trust we place in a company is an extension of our trust in how it operates, and that includes the tools it employs. There is no shortage of stories (some humorous, others troubling) covered in the popular press about an AI with untended outcomes. The more AI is deployed, however, and the more powerful it becomes, the more these stories will register with the broader public. Concerns will likely deepen, and an enterprise is well served by considering today how its AI endeavors will be guided such that they are deserving of customer trust.

To get there, we must go deeper than mere handwringing over nebulous ethical ideas. We need to get into the weeds of the components of trustworthy technology. And then, we must contemplate which elements of trust are most important in AI for our respective purposes.

A credit scoring AI tool that yields biased outputs is undeserving of trust, but fairness as an ethical concept does not apply to all AI tools. If a cognitive machine is trained to process invoices and remit payment, fairness and bias are irrelevant to the AI's proper function. Likewise, a credit scoring tool presents no real threat to personal safety, whereas the actions of a fast-moving robot arm in a factory are vitally important for safety. This is the landscape of trustworthy AI, and every organization must navigate it according to their needs and applications.

Thus, a point-for-point how-to on trustworthy AI is the red herring of AI application. Every business is entering this age with its own goals, strategies, technical capabilities, and risk tolerance. Legislators and regulators are increasingly wading into these ethical waters. And consumers are only now beginning to appreciate just how embedded AI is throughout every aspect of daily life. Every stakeholder on this frontier is charting a path to a bright horizon while attempting to anticipate the challenges in the way.

We can be sure that there will be missteps and blind spots. The ethical use of technology, like innovation itself, is not a straight line. Without serious consideration of all the potential outcomes, hubris and shortsightedness can be ingredients for unintended consequences. In 1922, Henry Ford wrote:

> We are entering an era when we shall create resources which shall be so constantly renewed that the only loss will be not to use them. There will be such a plenteous supply of heat, light and power, that it will be a sin not to use all we want.[2]

Now, a century later, such a statement is sobering in its error. It points to the question, what will be the outcomes from AI in the decades to come? Should we sprint into this future with the sentiment of using "all we want," or are we better served by dedicating effort now to guiding the trustworthiness of a technology we already know will change the world? As it is said, an ounce of prevention is worth a pound of cure. We have today an essential opportunity not just to prevent harm but to extract the greatest possible good from AI.

We have a grand opportunity to seize the moment and work toward the sociotechnical system that makes trustworthy AI possible. Given that so much of AI is developed and deployed by private enterprise, those who can affect the most positive impact are today's business leaders. From the boardroom of Fortune 100 companies to the local office of a small business, much of the future of AI rests in the capable hands of the private sector.

The Dimensions of Trustworthy AI

One of the unique challenges with creating trustworthy AI is that our definitions and ethics vary across cultures and geographies. There are also differences in social needs, environmental priorities, the nature of the AI application, and indeed, a near endless variety of conditions that defy a one-size-fits-all ethical framework for AI. In lieu of that, organizational leaders require subject-matter familiarity and a guidebook for operating in complex environments.

There are no standard answers in AI. The task is to ask the right questions and understand what to do with the answers. The path forward is paved with the dimensions of trust, broad philosophical and ethical areas where every enterprise must set its own speed limits and build its own traffic lights. In the public square, the notion of AI ethics is commonly conflated with bias, but this is just one aspect of the broader trustworthy tapestry. When we break apart the concept of trust, we find numerous dimensions, each with potential applicability to an AI use case.

Trustworthy AI is: fair and impartial; robust and reliable; respectful of privacy; safe and secure; responsible and accountable; and transparent and explainable. Each dimension commands its own qualities, challenges, and canon of philosophical inquiry. One of the tasks for those using AI today is to dig into these topics, understand what they mean, decide whether they are pertinent for a given use case, and if so, take appropriate action to preserve trust while capturing value. This is no simple task, one made more challenging by the breadth of stakeholders who should have a say in the overall effort of creating trustworthy, ethical AI.

This is not to suggest a tension between AI innovation, application, and ethics. It is not an either/or proposition, but it is an if/then imperative. When enterprise leaders embrace this view of AI, they are positioned to make thoughtful considerations of what is important and build and manage to the desired AI outcome. It is entirely possible to use AI that is explainable and safe. There are such things as reliable models that are simultaneously robust across use cases. Privacy and AI can exist in the same world.

But none of this will happen on its own. This book equips you with the bedrock ideas and questions that empower you to make the right decisions about how you use AI for business benefit. Not every dimension is applicable to every AI tool or use case, and there may be other dimensions that are relevant. As a starting point for wading into the trustworthy waters, the concepts and issues described in the ensuing chapters can help shape how people, processes, and technologies are harmonized to yield cognitive tools we can really trust.

Discoveries followed each other in rapid

succession, and it was obvious that a new

science was in course of development.

– Marie Curie

Chapter 1
A Primer on Modern AI

As a prelude to investigating the dimensions of AI trustworthiness, it is important to clarify what AI is – and what it is not. In popular press and general discussion, AI is often ascribed a sense of self, as if it "thinks" and even has a measure of "volition." The nouns we use to describe AI projects include "training" and "learning," concepts typically reserved for thinking creatures. Thus, it is perhaps unsurprising that common ways of talking about AI drift toward conceiving it as a true intellect.

This is quite far from reality. In truth, AI does not "think." AI tools are in fact highly complex mathematical calculations that have been constructed such that the solution to the calculations accurately describes something in the real world. More than this, AI as a concept is not just a discrete thing. It is as much a collection of model types performing different functions as it is a professional practice area for data scientists and the technology ecosystem that permits their work and the AI they develop.

To better define what we mean when we discuss AI, consider how the field developed to its current maturity and the kinds of AI models in use today.

The Road to Machine Intelligence

Humans have long imagined mechanical tools that act in a seemingly intelligent way. These ideas permeate the stories we tell, from those going back thousands of years to the ones we enjoy today. The automata created by Hephaestus in Greek myths, the mechanical beings in the Mahabharata and other ancient Hindu texts, the genre-defining fiction of Isaac Asimov and other writers – humans have always wondered about how inanimate machines might be given independent will that serves (and sometimes threatens) its creators.

When we discuss AI, one important step is delving into just what we mean by intelligence. Human beings have a clear sense of self and a rich internal world. Our decision making and knowledge owes to a pantheon of experience, intuition, superstition, emotion, and all the things that make us thinking creatures. AI as it is today is much narrower in its cognitive potential, accomplishing only what it is designed to do.

AI as a modern scientific field of study and practice emerged in the mid-twentieth century. It tracked the development of modern computer science, inspired and propelled in part by the work of British computer scientist Alan Turing. In the 1930s, Turing demonstrated mathematically that rules-based code could solve algorithmic problems, and it was he who developed the eponymous test for interrogating the presence of machine intelligence.

From those beginnings, the field of AI notched up a series of events and inflection points that moved the technology forward. At the 1956 Dartmouth Summer Research Project on Artificial Intelligence, researchers presented what has been dubbed the first AI program, Logic Theorist, and computer scientist John McCarthy coined the term "artificial intelligence." In the decades after, computer science and computational capabilities both evolved and improved. While there was heady excitement over what AI could potentially accomplish, however, the hardware, software, and algorithms were insufficiently powerful.

Over time, the technology advancements needed for AI, such as computer storage, steadily emerged. In the 1980s, deep learning techniques were devised, opening the door for machine learning (rather than purely rules-based code). While initially conceived in the 1950s, it took several decades for a type of AI called expert systems to mature. These used symbolic logic, data-driven processing, and outputs that could be understood beyond the realm of complex mathematics. The excitement was such that by the end of the 1980s, more than half of Fortune 500 companies were creating or using expert systems.[2] Yet, for a variety of reasons, including the technical and cognitive limits of expert systems, this avenue of AI fizzled out.

In the 1990s, neural networks received more technical innovation and more effective algorithms. Massively parallel processing also received research attention, seen most publicly in IBM's Deep Blue computer, which in 1997 beat the chess world champion in a six-game competition. Thus, it took nearly half a century to progress from the origin of the concept of AI to a technology that exceeded human performance in a highly complex activity.

At the turn of the century, the pace of development in computational infrastructure and capabilities quickened. The capabilities in data storage, parallel processing, and the data generation and connectivity permitted by the advent of the Internet all moved toward the computational power needed to make real the loftiest AI ambitions. Continued innovation around artificial neural networks made possible the potential for things like computer vision recognition, wherein a cognitive tool could accurately classify an object in an image. Yet, this type of AI and others like it were flummoxed by a fundamental issue – for machines to learn what an image contained, those images had to be labeled by a human.

For example, if there is a photo of a lion on the African savannah approaching a herd of gazelles, the machine learning tool has no sense of what is what. It does not know which is the lion and which is the gazelle, or even the concept of an animal in the wild. As such, lofty projects set out to hand-label every object in massive databases of images. This became prohibitively laborious.

Then, in 2011, deep learning emerged in full. Stanford computer scientist Andrew Ng and Google engineer Jeff Dean constructed a neural network, pairing it with a dataset of 10 million images and a cluster of 1,000 machines. They let algorithms process the raw data, and in three days, the cluster had independently created categories for human faces and bodies, as well as cat faces. This was proof that computers could generate feature detectors without labels. It was the advent of unsupervised learning.[3]

Over the last decade, these and other types of AI have proliferated and are being deployed at scale by organizations across every industry and sector. This has been aided by enormous generation of data through connected devices, flexibility in cloud computing, and the development of critical hardware (e.g., the graphics processing unit). Today, organizations are operating in a period of vigorous innovation and exploration. They seek not just to automate components of the enterprise but to totally reimagine how business is conducted and identify use cases that were never before possible. To be sure, AI is no longer a "nice to have." It is a competitive necessity.

Basic Terminology in AI

AI is not one thing; it is many things. It is an umbrella term for a variety of models, use cases, and supporting technologies. Importantly, the development of one machine learning technique does not necessarily make another obsolete. Rather, depending on use cases, there are a variety of AI techniques that may be most appropriate.

AI raises a highly technical lexicon that can be opaque to people outside of the data science field. The concepts in AI describe complex mathematics that can leave nontechnical people unsure of how AI actually works. There is no shortage of writing that probes and contests definitions in this evolving field. Yet, we do not need math to grasp the basics of AI. Definitions of relevant and often-referenced terms include:

Machine learning (ML) – At its most basic, ML consists of methods for automating algorithmic learning without human participation. The algorithm is supplied with data for training, and it independently "learns" to develop an approach to treating the data (based on whatever function the architect is optimizing). Machine learning methods might use both structured and unstructured data, though data processing for model training may inject some structure.

Neural network – An NN loosely models how a brain functions, in as much as it uses connected nodes to process and compute data. It is not a distinct physical object but instead the way computations are set up in a virtual space within a computer. An NN contains an input layer, an output layer, and a number of hidden layers between them. Each layer is composed of nodes and connections between nodes that together form a network of layers. Data is inserted into the input layer, computations are autonomously performed between hidden layers, and the algorithm produces an output.

Deep learning (DL) – A subset of ML, DL is largely (though not exclusively) trained with unstructured, unlabeled data. A DL algorithm uses a neural network to extract features from the data, refine accuracy, and independently adjust when encountering new data. The "deep" in DL refers to the number of layers in an NN. A challenge in DL is that as layers are added to the NN, the level of training error increases, and the task for data scientists is to adjust NN parameters until the algorithm is optimized to deliver an accurate output.

Supervised learning – In ML, one approach is to feed an algorithm labeled datasets. Humans curate and label the data before model training, and the model is optimized for accuracy with known inputs and outputs. In supervised learning, there are a variety of model types for classification (i.e., sorting data into appropriate categories) and for regression (probing relationships between variables).

Unsupervised learning – In this case, the training data is largely or entirely unlabeled and unstructured. The datasets are fed to an ML algorithm, and the model identifies patterns within the data, which it uses to reach an output that accurately reflects the real world. An example is the unsupervised learning approach Ng and Dean used in their 2011 image recognition experiment.

Reinforcement learning – Similar to how humans learn to act based on reward or reprimand, reinforcement learning is the ML approach where an algorithm optimizes its function by calculating an output and gauging the "reward," what could be simplistically called "trial and error."

While this list barely scratches the surface of AI vocabulary, it is sufficient for us to think critically about how AI training is conducted, how it can be applied, and where trust and ethics become important.

Types of AI Models and Use Cases

While there is a large degree of technical nuance and model variety, many of the AI tools used today can be categorized according to their basic operation and function. As a window into how AI is being used, review this sampling of AI functions and use cases:

Computer vision – AI cannot "see" anything, but a computer vision model can process the bits of data that together constitute a digital image and, from that, determine mathematically what is likely to be in the image. Today, this is possible not just with static pictures but also with real-time video. We see computer vision used in autonomous vehicles, facial recognition, equipment monitoring, and much more.

Natural language processing (NLP) – An NLP model can analyze, decipher, search, and generate language in the format humans use "naturally." The model does not "understand" language, but it can process and treat text such that the outputs are coherent and accurately reflect the data. These tools can classify, search, and create text. An example is an AI chatbot that can process a question from a customer and reply in a helpful way.

Speech recognition – Text-to-speech programs are nothing new, but AI adds a layer of knowledge. As words, intonation, and speech patterns are deciphered, speech recognition tools can analyze the sentiments of the person speaking. For example, is the person speaking expressing anger or joy, frustration or satisfaction? The way in which speech is delivered impacts the context and meaning of the words. Using sentiment analysis with an NLP model can yield a powerful tool that can compute not just what a person says but also what they mean.

Planning, scheduling, and predicting – In a complex organization, variables across business units and the speed at which conditions change can exceed human capacity to make fully informed decisions. Planning and scheduling were previously conducted by hand in spreadsheets. AI models today can offer granular insight across every business factor, supporting informed decision making and even predicting the likelihood of an issue occurring and recommending solutions to avoid or mitigate it.

Recommendation systems – With the growth of online shopping and media, the general public is aware of recommendation systems that serve up products, content, or offers that are relevant to the user. These models can become extraordinarily sophisticated when paired with information about the user, such as their shopping and travel habits, their age, income and education, and their online activity in social communities. Deep insight into consumer personas allows an organization to offer an individual or group the right content, offers, or advertisements in the format and timing most likely to be compelling.

Robotics – While not a distinct type of AI, cognitive tools are essential for semi- or fully autonomous robotics. Using AI to operate a physical object requires a collection of models and data that allow a robot to function in the real world. This may include computer vision but also monitoring machine performance, changes in the environment, and the degree of predictive certainty in given actions. We see these collections of AI in places such as manufacturing, autonomous vehicles, and consumer products (e.g., robot vacuums).

Ultimately, these types of AI are just a sampling of the true potential in cognitive tools. There is so much left to be conceived and invented, and excitement over and eagerness to use AI is fueling innovation, investment, experimentation, and progress. An appropriate question for any organization exploring AI is not just asking what the tool can do, but also, what the organization might do with it.

New Challenges for the Modern AI Era

When AI existed only in research labs and its potential was largely experimental, questions about trust and ethics were mostly academic. It is only when we deploy these powerful tools at scale that we are forced to contend with the unanswered questions about the ethics of AI and whether we can trust this bold new era of machine intelligence. As usually happens, our technology advancement has preceded the evolution of the sociotechnical system needed to govern it toward our collective best interests.

After decades of work and innovation, AI has matured to a point where it now touches almost every aspect of our lives. It is not a one-off research project that escaped the lab but instead *the* transformational technology that will shape our future. As such, armed with a general appreciation for what AI is and how it works, we can begin the serious work of exploring how to make this technology something we can trust.

One of the most important aspects of

any computing tool is its influence on the

thinking habits of those that try to use it.

– Edsger W. Dijkstra

Chapter 2
Fair and Impartial

L
ike many organizations, BAM Inc. was short on skilled labor. The enterprise had all the ingredients to improve its bottom line, but to get there, it needed more people working the factory floors. The Chief Human Resources Officer, Vidya, was constantly reminded that HR needed to increase the number of job candidates. The company needed people with the technical skills for high-precision machines, which required more brains than brawn.

To help dig through the mountain of resumes and applications, Vidya dusted off an AI system that had been moderately maintained but not used to its full extent. It was something her predecessor had brought into HR, and while Vidya preferred the traditional hands-on process of reviewing applications, there were just too many for her and her team to go through fast enough to satisfy immediate workforce needs.

Without much coordination with the data and AI teams, Vidya turned the system loose on the resumes, looking for the perfect people to work in their high-tech factories. Sure enough, resumes were flagged as deserving a closer look and consideration. It was just what they hoped for.

During an afternoon meeting, Vidya and the chief of operations were looking through potential hires.

"The AI made quick work of those applications," she said. "What are your thoughts?"

To which the operations chief said, "These are almost all men. That's odd. Are women not applying to work here? Seems like a missed talent pool."

At once, Vidya knew there was a problem.

There are numerous examples of how unfair, biased AI has led to harm and public backlash. Not only are end users hurt in some way, the organizations deploying AI also suffer consequences in the form of reputation damage, consumer trust, and legal implications. Government regulations for AI are increasing, as are the penalties for violations. In the United States, the Federal Trade Commission has pointed to existing laws covering AI-related applications and underscored that AI developers and users must adhere to specific laws, writing, "Hold yourself accountable – or be ready for the FTC to do it for you."[2]

AI application and potential are evolving so quickly across so many use cases that the onus for defining and pursuing fairness in AI often falls on the organizations that use it. With that, the way forward is paved with questions and ethical quandaries. Every use case and the impact on the end user is largely unique. The data, scientists, organizations, and real-world environments are so multifaceted that there is not (yet) a template to govern the development and deployment of fair AI.

Instead, as laws, regulations, and industry guidelines are crafted, organizations should understand where bias can emerge in the AI lifecycle. What are the components that contribute to unfair and biased AI? How can fairness in different use cases be assessed and addressed? Who are the stakeholders, and who holds the reins in steering AI toward fair application? As a starting point for understanding and mitigating bias in AI, we ask a more fundamental question: What is fairness?

A Longstanding Ethical Question

The meaning of fairness has been debated for thousands of years. Aristotle wrote in *Nicomachean Ethics* that "equals should be treated equally and unequals, unequally." The heart of fairness then is equal, impartial treatment. Considering that 2,000 years after Aristotle we still see inequity in every nation and market-place tells us that achieving fairness is not just difficult but also tenuous and even fleeting.

With the premise that fairness is rooted in equal treatment, consider notions of procedural and distributive fairness, which extends beyond equal *treatment* and looks to equal *outcomes*. Procedural fairness (that is, equal treatment, as Aristotle viewed it) refers to how procedures, if followed, lead to fair outcomes and the related concept of justice. Philosopher John Rawls wrote about three tiers of procedural justice:[3]

1. **Perfect procedural justice** – Given a concrete definition of fairness, there is a procedure that guarantees a fair outcome every time.
2. **Imperfect procedural justice** – With a fixed procedure, a fair outcome is likely, but there is no guarantee.
3. **Pure procedural justice** – A fair outcome is that which results from the procedure, but there is no independent definition of what is fair; it is merely consistent via the procedure.

For AI, defining what is fair for all use cases is frustrated by the fact that new AI use cases are constantly arising. That which is "fair" in an intrinsic sense remains highly subjective, depending on the application and the impact. Pure procedural justice is that the outcome is fairly arrived at because the procedure is consistent and that underpins the notion of equal treatment. This points to distributive justice – are the outcomes equal, and if so, is that fair?

Consider an AI tool used to facilitate hiring, which scans resumes and scores the job applicants. In theory, such a tool would help remove personal bias when deciding whom to hire, while also expediting the process of finding the best potential employees. In practice, however, if the training dataset contains bias toward a given gender, the resulting AI may penalize resumes from applicants of that gender, thus resulting in biased hiring decisions.

In this example, the AI tool can be seen as both procedurally and distributively unfair. The process by which job candidates are scored is biased and that inevitably leads to unfair outcomes. This reveals the importance of fairness of allocation and quality of service. AI can permit or restrict equal access to opportunity, such as being considered for a job or receiving a mortgage. It can also enable or diminish equal treatment in services.

An additional component organizations should weigh is that no matter how transparent the data science underlying an AI model, it will likely remain opaque and difficult to understand by the people who are impacted by the outputs. Ethical human behavior is guided by prosocial reasoning, through which individuals understand, evaluate, and move toward positive social behavior by interacting with others. We intuitively know what is fair and impartial in the context of our society by interacting with peers, and antisocial behaviors are naturally marginalized through the function of society. Importantly, which behaviors are deemed antisocial can vary between communities and societies. Explicit or implicit bias might be tolerated or even enforced in some cases.

In any case, however, machines cannot intuit what is fair or "think" through why it might be. Concerns over AI fairness have birthed a new discipline, algorithmic fairness, which is focused on exploring how to remove bias and promote equity in the use of data, analytics, and AI. While one path is blinding algorithms to sensitive attributes like gender, ethnicity, and age, another is to carefully include those data points (where laws, regulations, and common sense permit).[4]

These are complicated matters with considerations far beyond data science. Fairness carries different meaning depending on the subject matter. There are tomes written about fairness in law, business, social structures, math, and much more. This is perhaps why fairness and impartiality can be so difficult to nail down. When it comes to AI, rather than establishing rigid definitions, it is valuable to step back and identify a specific problem vis-à-vis AI fairness and approach the challenge in that way. One fundamental component is understanding and then addressing bias.

The Nature of Bias in AI

Bias is a human feature – it's part what makes humans human. There are dozens of identified cognitive biases that influence human behavior. There is the post-purchase rationalization bias, where one persuades oneself that something they bought is of high value, regardless of whether it is. Take the "IKEA effect," through which people perceive greater value in something they assemble themselves, no matter the quality of the ultimate object. And the "Gambler's fallacy," where the probability of some future occurrence (winning) is judged by past occurrences (losing), even though the odds are unchanged.

AI is free from most of these illogical biases, but it is susceptible bias that makes its outputs potentially unfair and untrustworthy. The root of AI bias is buried in the data. Bias in this context can have a narrow meaning, referring to the difference between the predicted and actual output values from the training data. Bias might also mean that the data reflects bias that is embedded in our society, influencing the way we collect data on characteristics such as gender, race, or socioeconomic status. And bias in data science can emerge when datasets are inaccurate reflections of the real world. This does not always mean that human behavior is at fault. A malfunctioning machine sensor, for example, can output data that is incomplete or incorrect. A dataset's files could be corrupted in storage due to a technical failure.

In many other instances, human behavior does impact the quality and accuracy of the data. This is not necessarily a reflection of malicious intent or neglect on the part of the data scientist. Data bias can arise from a variety of social and institutional trends that persist despite running counter to our notions of fairness (e.g., the likelihood for men to more often hold managerial positions than women because gender bias influences promotions). And while understanding the roots of bias may seem on its face to be largely academic, the results of biased data and AI can have profound impacts in the business world.

One famous example is revealed in a *ProPublica* investigation that found that an algorithm used across the United States for scoring a criminal's recidivism risk was yielding racially biased outputs.[5] White defendants were incorrectly given a low risk score more often than Black defendants, and Black defendants were erroneously scored as likely to commit future crimes at nearly twice the rate for White defendants. While risk scores were only meant to be a component of how sentences were determined, the implications for this kind of bias are vast as one bad output could impact a person's life for years.

With this, AI teams should look deeply into the data and into their own perspectives to help mitigate and even prohibit bias. From a business lens, let's focus on four key biases.

Selection Bias

Data collection is never perfect. There will always be some aspect of the data where details are missing or over- or underrepresented. Imagine a simple survey of people passing on a sidewalk and how bias can be baked into a dataset because of how it is collected. Are the people on the street a truly representative sample? Are some people more or less likely to agree to participate? Is the surveyor more likely to approach one person over another? The bias inherent in the data gathering means the dataset is also biased, and without any mitigating steps, so too will be the AI model trained on it.

A complicating factor for AI development is that the data used is often from secondary sources, that is, information resulting from an activity unrelated to AI modeling. This might be sales data, data from after-market product use, or conversion rates for advertising campaigns. With secondary data, scientists might have minimal visibility into how the data was collected and whether it is an accurate representation of people and activities.

Lurking in the data might be what is called passive selection bias, where aspects of the data are underrepresented. Take the surveyor on the street – they may be failing to collect information from important cohorts by virtue of where they are asking the questions. Would the dataset change measurably if the questioner went to a different neighborhood or city?

Meanwhile, active selection bias refers to data collection that oversamples one aspect of the dataset while undersampling or excluding another. The surveyor may be collecting feedback about a product that is more often used by men than by women and so incidentally records more input from men who have an opinion on it than from women who do not.

And with all this there is the potential for self-selection bias, in which a cohort is underrepresented in the data because they elect not to provide that data. All of these kinds of selection biases can yield a dataset that is not a true representative sample, and the data scientist using that data (particularly if it is secondary data) may be challenged to identify where the bias resides and to what degree.

Confirmation Bias

People are susceptible to seeking out and trusting information that confirms their existing beliefs and rejecting information that contradicts them. This confirmation bias influences popular media and arguments we tend to favor, such as watching one news channel over another or participating in a social media circle that supports our thinking rather than challenges it. This is how social media echo chambers can grow and persist.

In research, confirmation bias can arise intentionally or unintentionally. If a scientist puts forward a hypothesis, they have already established what they think could be true and so they may guide their research to support a theory that aligns with their thinking. The unethical scientist might obscure or ignore information to make their theory appear correct, but more likely, they subconsciously focus on information that supports their hypothesis.

When it comes to data science, confirmation bias is looking for connections and patterns that fit a predetermined hypothesis, which results in a false prediction. In AI training, a data scientist might amend or reshape data to yield a model that meets the desired output, but the implications are that the AI tool might not be viable and accurate when deployed in the real world.

Explicit and Implicit Bias

Conscious or explicit bias (i.e., prejudice) is a known bias toward something or someone. Racist and bigoted beliefs, for example, may be known to the person who holds them, but the bias could extend to more benign views, such as a belief that autonomous vehicles will without doubt replace human drivers, no matter any dissenting argument. In the context of AI, while a data scientist could hold a conscious bias, it is perhaps easier to prohibit in model development, deployment, and operation because that bias is known to them.

More challenging to mitigate is unconscious or implicit bias, views that someone holds but is unaware that those views are present and influencing decision making. As an example, social psychologists Dr. Jennifer Eberhardt and Dr. Jason Okonofua studied the difference in how K–12 teachers respond to misbehavior in the classroom depending on the student's ethnicity.[6] What they found was that teachers were more likely to view repeated disobedience from Black students as severe and deliver harsher discipline for it relative to the White students. The insight was that a teacher's unconscious bias influenced how they viewed student behavior.

For data science, unconscious bias can influence every step of the AI lifecycle. The data collection could be influenced by an unconscious bias, the scientists could make design decisions based on implicit bias, and the operation and interpretation of outputs could be shaped by an unrecognized bias. And more challenging still, the data could contain latent bias, which is a longstanding stereotype that influences the data itself. For example, a natural language processing (NLP) algorithm may be trained on a dataset that ties "CEO" to "male" and "secretary" to "female." This specific type of gender bias is all too common in NLP because the datasets on which models are trained contain latent bias.[7] The result is that the AI is inherently biased in the way it associates gender and professional roles.

Institutional Bias

Some components of modern society have bias embedded so deeply in systems and mores that they almost go unrecognized. People can face bias due to a range of protected attributes, like gender, ethnicity, age, and sexual orientation, and those engrained biases can show up in the data and influence AI models. When the foundational data on which models are trained includes institutional bias, the output of that AI will reflect it.

Take, for example, a common use for AI in law enforcement. Predicting where crime will occur has great value for public safety, and an algorithm can be used to analyze historical crime data and infer where crime might occur in the near future. Some police departments have taken this approach, using AI to guide where patrols are focused, with the intention of inhibiting crime by their presence or responding faster to an incident. The allure is that because the data used is only historical and does not include protected attributes like race, policing can be less influenced by officer bias.[8]

However, if the historical data informing the algorithm is itself reflective of a history of biased policing in certain communities, the resulting AI remains tied to that institutional bias and can even perpetuate it. What is more, this can create a feedback loop. Imagine that an algorithm predicts crime will occur in a specific area of a city, and police respond by sending more officers to patrol. With more officers there, more arrests might be made than otherwise, and so the algorithm potentially becomes more likely to indicate high crime in that area, leading to a higher police presence. This runaway effect yields an ineffective application of limited resources, but it also exposes law enforcement organizations to (valid) challenges that its strategies are biased and unfair.

Looking across the types of bias, the challenge of ensuring that AI delivers fair outcomes becomes clearer. There is not one point of failure that can be addressed with a simple fix to process or education. The collage of biases creates a thicket of subjectivity in people and data that present a significant hurdle for organizations deploying AI. Enterprises are focused on delivering products or services, but with AI, they must address philosophical questions and complicated ethical considerations far outside the realm of day-to-day business. Are they equipped to do so? Do they have the time, resources, and wherewithal? Laws and regulations will compel the effort, but it does not simplify the challenge.

Perhaps to the good then that not every AI use case hinges on an absolute achievement of unbiased data and design. Indeed, some AI biases are necessary for their function, and what's needed is a balance between the least amount of bias and the most effective AI tool.

Back at BAM Inc., CHRO Vidya knew the application-screening AI system was operating incorrectly. Looking through the records of its operation, she saw that it had rejected almost every resume submitted by a woman. It made no sense. There were dozens of high-quality candidates with rich experience and excellent education. Where had the AI system gone so wrong?

Rejecting applications based on gender was not just a detriment to the workforce. It also exposed the enterprise to potential discrimination lawsuits. If an eager journalist uncovered the issue, it could be a public relations disaster for the company. And if a regulatory body zeroed in, there could be real penalties. So much was going wrong because the system favored applications from men.

Perplexed and disheartened, Vidya joined her old friend Frank, who after a long tenure as an operations manager for BAM Inc. had retired and sat on an advisory board for the company. Frank often spoke about how much had changed in manufacturing, reflecting on how his predecessors had been in the dangerous business of moving molten steel and working with huge machines. He went on: "Of course, this was back in the days when society had the silly notion that only men could work in manufacturing and women worked in less physically demanding roles. Maybe if we'd had more diversity, we could have come up with a better way to do things."

Vidya sat up straighter as an idea flickered. AI is trained on data. How old was their data? Was that the root of bias?

Tradeoffs in Fairness

With data that is potentially biased, there is a tradeoff for the algorithm. It can be highly accurate in operation, relative to the data, but that can lead to unjust outcomes. For example, an AI tool trained on historical data with inherent racial biases can operate exactly as the data instructs, as if it were a perfect representation of the real world, but the outcome would likely perpetuate the bias in the data. In driving toward statistical parity, where outcomes are even across all groups, the data bias must be mitigated, which can lead to lower algorithmic accuracy but higher statistical parity. This can become more complicated still with varying types of fairness, where research suggests not all can be simultaneously satisfied.[9]

Ultimately, machine learning is not possible without some inherent bias, and that is not always a bad thing. Imagine an AI tool that processes health records to determine risk for breast cancer, which occurs much more commonly in women than in men. It makes no sense to adjust the dataset to achieve statistical parity whereby risk is determined without regard to gender. Gender in this example is an essential data point for risk scoring.

Therein is the realization that AI requires human participation and judgment. An algorithm is simply a powerful and complex computation whose result informs human decision making. It cannot replace the essential judgment of deciding what *fair* means in the context of the use case and to what degree the AI outputs can or should be trusted to be fair. This moves the application of AI out of the narrow role of the data scientist and into a wider group of stakeholders, like ethicists and domain experts.

A concept of fairness is never black and white, and it may be more important in some applications than in others. Fairness is likely less important to an AI tool for seizing efficiencies in the supply chain, but it is vitally important in cases where the tool directly impacts people's lives, such as having equal access to loans, insurance, social services, educational opportunities, and much more.[10] It is a human task to consider the relevance of fairness for a use case, and if the risk from unfairness outweighs the benefits, then that calls for business decision making.

In this, we are looking increasingly at the ethics not of the machine but of the people who sponsor, design, build, and operate it. This is a heavy responsibility for data scientists, who operate in a world of calculations and may lack the time and background to drive the collective reasoning to make important judgment calls. The challenge only compounds as organizations deploy dozens or even hundreds of AI tools.

Who will make the decisions? A Chief AI Ethics Officer? A board charged with investigating use cases? What does fairness mean to them in the context of their industry? What risks must they weigh in pursuit of benefits for the enterprise and the end user? Expecting a data science team to both build models and ensure they adhere to subjective ethical concepts can be a recipe for poor outcomes and costly consequences for the business. In this, it becomes clear that achieving fairness should be a shared responsibility between business leaders and data scientists.

Put AI to the Test on Fairness

- Does your organization have the right AI policies, controls, and related data to avoid discrimination and bias? What controls do you need to ensure your algorithms maintain fairness?
- Does the algorithm display discriminatory bias toward certain groups? Is differential treatment of groups justified by underlying factors? How do you know and test this?
- How does your organization evaluate and monitor the data used? What is the source of the data? Is the data a fair representation of the relevant population?
- How do you respond if a lack of fairness is detected?
- Will customers trust that the outputs are fair? How do you know?
- How would your organization defend its positions on AI fairness before elected officials, a regulator, a court, or a concerned public?
- Has your organization thought about worst-case scenarios and possible reputational damage from unfair AI?
- Has your organization considered risks related to its third-party partners with which it is developing/deploying AI solutions?

Leading Practices in Promoting Fairness

Driving toward fairness requires looking for bias within the data, as well as in the thinking of the teams who design and deploy

AI models. Leading practices in promoting fair and impartial AI include:

Build a Diverse Team

Different lived experiences yield unique insights that cannot be taught. With this, an enterprise's AI team, as well as stakeholders engaged in using AI, should be diverse. A variety of people can better engage in collective reasoning that results in fairer decisions that keep the end user in mind. Collaboration should be not just encouraged but structured. Each phase of the AI lifecycle should include benchmarks for evaluating fairness, as well as internal and external audits and checks embedded in processes to enable a diversity of people to continuously monitor and validate AI fairness.

Balance the Datasets

In data collection and curation, oversampling can balance datasets such that they contain sufficient information for an algorithm to yield fair outputs. If a researcher is collecting economic data for a given neighborhood and the demographics of that neighborhood are skewed, such as being predominantly inhabited by white residents, a truly representative sample requires more data from minority residents such that race does not introduce disparity into the dataset, which could have known and unknown implications for AI fairness.

Data scientists might also weight some data more than others to account for inputs that are not equally represented (while being careful not to inadvertently introduce new bias by overcompensating). Or they may use synthetic data to compensate for missing sample data, producing a more balanced dataset for model training. Existing datasets, such as secondary sources, can also be probed using stratified samples. If there are enough distinct variables where data points can be sorted into strata, it can enable truer random sampling, since an accidental over- or underrepresentation becomes less likely with this technique.

Probe the Data

What if a bias is unknown? Exploratory data analysis refers to probing the data to look for variables that might be introducing bias. If the data is categorical, one approach is cross-tabulation. This means correlating variables and looking for anomalies. Correlation matrix analysis takes this a step further by computing the correlation between two variables. It can yield deeper insights that are valuable for AI model building, but it can also make odd correlations stand out, helping guide the data scientists as they explore the dataset for bias.

Engage AI Stakeholders

These technical approaches are only part of the challenge. As shown, the people working with the data and models are also potential sources of bias. Data scientists may or may not know of their biases, and all people may be blind to institutional bias that is so engrained it is nearly invisible. Mitigating steps are training and education to reflect on one's thinking and identify biases that could influence AI fairness.

Develop Pathways for Feedback and Evaluating Performance

Recognizing the potential for bias to linger in models despite these leading practices and efforts, the organization should also develop processes and controls focused on receiving and exploring feedback from the variety of end users. In assessing fairness in quality of service, for example, evaluate performance metrics for underrepresented groups. This requires test metrics across the entire test set, as well as for each group categorized by sensitive attributes.

These kinds of approaches to addressing bias move directly toward developing and deploying AI that is fair and impartial, delivering anticipated business value while also upholding the ethical imperative.

Toward a Fairer Future in AI

CHRO Vidya called an emergency meeting with BAM Inc.'s scientists, AI managers, and dedicated advisors. She had just one question: Did the training data for the application-screening AI favor men for certain positions at the company? After investigating the data and applying probing algorithms, Vidya had her answer.

The dataset reflected the erroneous conclusion that only men of a certain age and background were suited for factory floor work because it was physically demanding. This revealed an inherent bias buried so deep it was difficult to see. The dataset suggested, "Women are not as strong and therefore cannot do this job."

Not only was this bias thoroughly wrong just on its merits, it also was well astray of what the enterprise truly needed for its workforce. The required strengths had nothing to do with how much a person could lift. It was almost exclusively about the quality of their thought and decision making. Vidya instructed the data science team to find better representative data, and the AI engineers took up the task of retraining the model from the ground up.

This kind of scenario plays out across numerous industries with varying characteristics and qualities embedding bias in AI function. Yet, unlike at BAM Inc., fairness is rarely a black-or-white proposition. More than that, it is not always a relevant ethical concern for an AI use case.

Most challenging are instances where fairness *might* be relevant, depending on how data is used and impacts individuals. In healthcare, for example, sensitive attributes like race and gender are necessary for AI to support treatment, such as when predicting the likelihood that a patient will develop a malady (e.g., sickle cell anemia is more prevalent among people with African genetic heritage). The dataset must include personal attributes, but does it also need to include, for example, patient ZIP codes? Could that introduce an unintended bias that leads to unfair AI?

These gray areas where the ethical question is answered with "maybe" are where data scientists and organizational leaders should think critically about the relationship between bias, fairness, and AI accuracy. The implications for balancing these issues are significant for the organization deploying AI, for the effects on people and businesses, and for the future of AI itself. Whether AI reaches its full potential depends on the choices we make today in building world-changing tools with significant potential impacts on society.

In this, organizations are obligated to define what fairness means in the context of an AI use case and their business and to take a genuine interest in building tools that don't just work for the business but work for the interests of all. There are hard consequences for failing to do so, like fines and brand damage, but there is a virtuous cause as well. When longstanding biases that plague datasets are understood, identified, and expunged, it can begin to shift society and systems forward and toward a more equitable future.

Right now the new is you, but someday

not too long from now, you will gradually

become the old and be cleared away.

– Steve Jobs

Chapter 3
Robust and Reliable

At BAM Inc., Mariam was having calibration problems and customers were complaining. The parts coming out of two manufacturing plants in Vietnam were sub-par. Shipments were being returned, costs were rising, and Mariam could not figure out why those plants were having so many problems.

She had already dug through the local processes, the human talent, the management approach, and a dozen other things that could be causing the problem. And as she was considering the timeline of this poor performance, it dawned on her: the problems started after they deployed the AI system that executed calibration on one type of high-precision grinding machine.

What was mystifying was that the machines abroad were all identical, as were the AI systems. The German plants manufactured to customer specifications, as did the North American plants. Why would the AI system work everywhere except in Vietnam? It was a question that demanded an answer, as more shipments came back and the complaints piled up in her inbox.

With AI model training, datasets are a proxy for the real world. Models are trained on one dataset and tested against another, and if the results are similar, there is an expectation that the model functions can translate to the operational environment. What works in the lab *should* work consistently in the real world, but for how long? Perfect operating scenarios are rare in AI, and real-world data is messy and complex. This has led to what leading AI researcher Andrew Ng called a "proof-of-concept-to-production gap," where models train as desired but fail once they are deployed.[2] It is partly a problem of robustness and reliability.

When outputs are inconsistently accurate and become worse over time, the result is uncertainty. Data scientists are challenged to build provably robust, consistently accurate AI models in the face of changing real-world data. In the information flux, the algorithm can meander away, with small changes in input cascading into large shifts in function.

To be sure, not all tools operate in environments prone to dramatic change, and not all AI models present the same levels of risk and consequence if they become inaccurate or undependable. The task for enterprises as they grow their AI footprint is to weigh robustness and reliability as a component of their AI strategy and align the processes, people, and technologies that can manage and correct for errors in a dynamic environment.

To that end, we start with some of the primary concepts in the area of robust and reliable AI.

Robust vs Brittle AI

The International Organization for Standardization defines AI robustness as the "ability of an AI system to maintain its level of performance under any circumstances."[3] In a robust model, the training error rate, testing error rate, and operational error rate are all nearly the same. And when unexpected data is encountered in operation or when the model is operating in less-than-ideal conditions, the robust AI tool continues to deliver accurate outputs.

For example, if a model can identify every image of an airplane in a training dataset and is proven to perform at a high level on testing data, then the model *should* be able to identify airplane pictures in any dataset, even if it has not encountered them previously. But how does the airplane-identifying model perform if a plane is pink, photographed at dusk, missing a wing or viewed at an angle? Does its performance degrade, and if so, at what point is the model no longer viable?

When small changes in the environment lead to large changes in functionality and accuracy, a model is considered inelastic or "brittle." Brittleness is a known concept in software engineering, and it is apt for AI as well. Ultimately, all AI models are brittle to some degree. The different kinds of AI tools we use are specific to their function and their application. AI does only what we train it to do.

There is another component to this. Those deploying and managing AI must weigh how changing real-world data leads to degrading model accuracy over time. In the phenomenon of "model drift," the predictive accuracy of an AI tool decreases as the underlying variables that inform the model change. Signals and data sources that were once trusted can become unreliable. Unexpected malfunctions in a network can lead to changes in data flows.

An AI that plays chess is likely to remain robust over time, as the rules of chess and the moves the AI will encounter are predictable and static. Conversely, a natural language processing (NLP) chatbot operates in the fluid landscape of speech patterns, colloquial language, incorrect grammar and syntax, and a variety of changing factors. With machine learning, unexpected data or incorrect computations can lead a model astray, and what begins as a robust tool deteriorates to brittleness, unless corrective tactics are employed.

Developing Reliable AI

The European Commission's Joint Research Centre notes that assessing reliability requires consideration of performance and vulnerability.[4] Reliable AI performs as expected even given inputs that were not included in training data, what are called out-of-distribution (OOD) inputs. These are data points that are different from the training set, and reliable AI must be able to detect whether data is OOD. One challenge is that for some models, OOD inputs can be classified with high confidence, meaning the AI tool is ostensibly reliable when in fact it is not.

Take an autonomous delivery robot. Its navigation AI is optimized to find the most direct path to its destination. The training dataset has all the example data the AI needs to recognize sidewalks, roads, crosswalks, curbs, pedestrians, and every other variable – *except* railroad tracks intersecting a pathway. In operation, the robot identifies rail tracks in its path, and while they are OOD, the AI computes high confidence that the tracks are just a new kind of footpath, which it follows to expedite its delivery. Clearly, the AI has gone astray due to an OOD input. If it is not hit by a train, it validates for the delivery robot, "This is a viable path" and may look for other rail tracks to use. And the operators may be none the wiser – until a train comes along.

Reliable AI is accurate in the face of any novel input. This is different from average performance. A model that offers good average performance may still yield occasional outputs with significant consequences, hampering reliability. If an AI tool is accurate 80% of the time, is it a trustworthy model? A related matter is resilience to vulnerabilities, be they natural outcomes from operation or the result of adversarial exploits.

The Challenge of Generalizable Deep Learning

The subset of machine learning known as deep learning has led to powerful innovations and AI applications transforming industries and business models. Deep learning works in part by identifying patterns in data to perform calculations in such a way that the system outputs what it was trained and intended to do.

Humans can identify patterns, understand correlations between objects, and develop semantic meaning by virtue of it. We know since childhood: hot things hurt to touch, the pan is hot and will hurt if I touch it, and the burner beneath the pan is emitting heat, which makes the pan hot.

This is way beyond the cognitive capabilities of any current AI. AI tools might extrapolate correlation between data points, but they struggle to determine causation.

In a factory, a robotic arm controlled by an AI is trained to take manufactured widgets off of a conveyor belt and place them into a box. The AI is finely tuned to grasp and move one kind of object in one orientation in a static environment. For humans, we intuitively understand that grasping and moving objects with our arm applies to all objects in all scenarios. But for the robot arm, if the widget changes shape, if the conveyor belt moves faster, if the machine itself is set a foot higher or lower, the tool's accuracy may degrade or suffer a catastrophic failure. How much more impossible would it be for the robot to generalize its grasping function to meaningfully different applications, such as moving dirty dishes into a washer or placing groceries into a car trunk? Importantly, the AI-controlled robot arm may be more robust than a purely rules-driven, hard-programmed equivalent, but functioning more robustly than the alternative does not on its own engender trust or support generalizable functions.

Part of the challenge is that AI systems do not "understand" the tasks they accomplish. Unlike humans, AI lacks an internal model of the world. The robot arm exists in a universe composed entirely of widgets and boxes. There are no dishes or groceries, and it has no concept of grasping and moving as a general capability. As models move from training data to test data to real-world data, they need to be elastic enough to remain accurate despite perturbations in the data and environment, and they must do so without any real sense of why.

An AI tool's robustness or brittleness depends in part on whether it is transferable to applications in not just fluctuating but also suboptimal environments. A facial recognition tool that gives accurate outputs when using a high definition CCTV system may become less accurate if it is reapplied to a lower definition video system. The data feeding in is of poorer quality, the tool's function degrades, and the model is less transferable and more brittle.

Ongoing research is advancing the capacity of AI tools to be generalizable. There are platforms and robotics that can be trained for accuracy and capabilities across a range of environments. Yet, in the end, once trained, the models are still vulnerable to model, data, and concept drifts, leading inevitably to brittleness. The task is to train models to perform as reliably and consistently as possible, for as long as needed.

Factors Influencing AI Reliability

In her quest to determine why some foreign plants were producing poor products, BAM Inc.'s engineering chief Mariam dug into the data. She called on the data engineers who selected and curated the datasets, and she also spoke with the data scientists who trained the model. She talked with the plant managers in Vietnam, who were just as upset as she. They had been running smoothly until the AI system was deployed globally.

There was a mismatch, somewhere, between the training data, the real-world environment, and the AI performance. Mariam just had to find it.

On a dreary summer evening, Mariam drove home after another day unable to crack the mystery. The air was unusually damp for that time of year, and the inside of her car's windshield and windows were foggy. She fumbled with the recirculation button to blow cool air and defog the glass—and she froze.

Humidity.

Mariam pulled a hard U-turn and raced back to her office.

What Mariam was cluing in on is a central challenge in building and using robust and reliable AI. To probe this issue, there are valuable insights from computer science that can help. Two related areas are data reliability and reliability engineering. Concepts from each offer a window into priorities and challenges in AI reliability.

Lessons in Data Reliability

The quality of a model is only as good as the training and testing data used to develop it. Without confidence in the data quality vis-à-vis its representation of the real world, the model's outputs may not reliably deliver accurate outputs in the operational environment. For the U.S. Government Accountability Office,[5] data reliability hinges on:

- Applicability – Does the data provide valid measures of relevant qualities?

- Completeness – To what degree is the dataset populated across all attributes?
- Accuracy – Does the data reflect the real world from which the dataset was gathered?

These are cross-cutting components of trustworthy data, as well as AI. Datasets need to be sufficiently curated and in some cases labeled or even supplemented with synthetic data, which can compensate for missing data points or fill in for protected information that cannot (or should not) be used in training. Data must also be scrubbed for latent bias, which skews model training and leads to undesirable outputs or predictions.

As with the AI tool itself, real-world operational data needs to be monitored for shifting trends and emerging data science needs. For example, a model conducting sentiment analysis may be trained to score sentiment across a dozen variables, but after deployment, the AI team identifies other variables that need to be accounted for in model drift and retraining.

Like reliability, data applicability is not static. Likewise, data accuracy might fluctuate based on how well sensors perform, whether there are latency or availability issues, or any of the known factors that can hamper data reliability.

Meeting the Long Tail in Reliability Engineering

A common sentiment in site reliability engineering is that when you increase scale, you meet the long tail. Consider an AI model with high average performance accuracy that performs as desired during testing and once deployed. Yet, reliable outputs in development are no guarantee of total reliability once deployed and then over time. As AI tools scale and their impact grows, the lingering possibility of inaccuracy compounds (i.e., the "tail").

For some AI systems where reliability is vital, just a few bad outputs can have catastrophic outcomes. As an example, there are growing AI capabilities in disease detection. The promise of AI in medicine is profound, but in life-and-death situations, is a high average performance sufficiently reliable? Inconsistent reliability may be an acceptable shortcoming if AI performance exceeds human judgment (such as in identifying malignant growths in radiology scans). But in other cases (such as robot-assisted surgery), what's needed is near-total reliability, irrespective of novel or OOD inputs. As with all AI use cases, the organization deploying the tool should calculate for itself the importance of AI reliability relative to AI value.

Engineering reliability in machine learning requires a complete end-to-end view of systems, such that model outcomes can be justified through an independent approach. This includes understanding technology infrastructure, data collection and management, model analysis, and more. With a comprehensive understanding of the factors and functionality involved in AI training and management, the data science team can mitigate and monitor the potential problems with reliability that can emerge when tools are deployed at scale.

Robustness and Bad Actors

AI tools are deployed into a real-world environment full of threats to safety and security. One element of robustness is whether a model can continue to deliver accurate outputs in the face of what are called "adversarial examples." These are data inputs introduced by bad actors that can trick a model into delivering an inaccurate output.

Take an image recognition system that is trained to identify farm animals. If an attacker understands how the system works and how to trick it, it is possible to take a picture of a horse and insert perturbations so slight at the pixel level that the changes are indistinguishable to the human eye. While visually similar to humans, for the AI model, the arithmetic values of the original and perturbed images are quite close, leading the system to misidentify a chicken as a cow.

This kind of threat to AI robustness is a reflection of the familiar "knowledge" problem. The image recognition system has no common sense around why a small bird with a beak is different from a large mammal with hooves. It does not even understand what an animal is. The underlying algorithm is pure math, and image pixels adjusted in just the right way in an adversarial example can make an AI (with high confidence) mistake a cow for a chicken.

Instances of adversarial examples from bad actors are not often widely reported, but these attacks do happen, and for some applications, the consequences can be severe. The techniques for building systems that are robust against adversarial examples are still formative.[6] Organizations should weigh the value of AI and the capacity to mitigate risks.

Consequences Worth Contemplating

Good questions to ask of every AI application are, how important is accuracy and how safety-critical is the system? AI accuracy is tough and fleeting, and deploying a model necessarily comes with considerations around risk, reward, and consequence.

Some AI applications present trivial or low-cost consequences for inaccuracy. A speech recognition system transcribing a city town hall meeting has a low consequence for misidentifying some words. If the system is accurate 80% of the time, that may be sufficient for the local needs and so the robustness of the system is appropriate.

With other applications, however, the cost of inaccuracy is substantial and robustness is critical. For systems whose outputs have life-and-death implications, AI reliability is enormously important. An autonomous vehicle that avoids pedestrians 80% of the time is not a vehicle that can be trusted. Likewise, if a system that detects skin cancer provides higher accuracy rates for men over women, that is not only potentially life-threatening for some patients, it also engenders (rightfully) deep mistrust in the application of AI in healthcare.

Meanwhile, the network of systems that increasingly underpin business functions can have major impacts on the bottom line. Predictive supply chain management can become wildly inaccurate, potentially threatening business operations. A product lifecycle management tool could push a software update to all end users, only to cause system-breaking bugs on many devices. Employee scheduling, asset valuation, production errors, talent recruitment, customer engagement – indeed, wherever an AI system is deployed, robustness is a factor, and the higher value the use case, the greater the ramifications from its inaccuracy and/or failure.

In high-stakes use cases, enterprises deploying brittle AI may also expose the organization to regulatory or legal consequences. Catastrophic failures or costly repercussions for inaccuracies could bring fines, civil suits, and possibly criminal liability. There is also a risk of reputation damage in the marketplace, diminished internal buy-in for future AI initiatives, and the potential for individual consequences for business leaders in the form of stunted advancement or termination.

Put Your AI to the Test on Robustness and Reliability

- Can your organization's AI systems perform as intended in less than ideal conditions and when encountering unexpected situations and data? Will the algorithm produce reliable results with each new set of data?
- Are appropriate controls in place during the development of the model such that it is developed as intended? What process needs to be in place when inconsistencies or issues are discovered?
- Can your organization sufficiently monitor its AI systems?
- For complex AI systems that have business-critical impacts, does your organization have plans to address deficiencies in a time-sensitive manner?
- How much human input is required to ensure reliability, at which points in the process is that input needed, and who provides the input?
- Are those providing input equipped to take on this responsibility? Are they trained on company guidelines and policies?

Leading Practices in Building Robust and Reliable AI

Whether a model is hampered by unfamiliar data, perturbed by a malicious actor, or drifting from accuracy, organizations should embed within their AI initiatives the capacity to evaluate risk of deployment, track performance to intended specifications, gauge (if not measure) robustness, and have the processes in place to fix failing or drifting models as their reliability degrades. Because reliability flows out of robustness, some of the activities that can contribute to AI reliability include:

Benchmarks for Reliability

Even while model training is ongoing, identify and define which benchmarks are most valuable for tracking and measuring reliability. The benchmarks might include how the AI system performs relative to human performance, which is particularly apt given that deep learning models attempt to mimic human cognition.[7]

Perform Data Audits

As a component of testing, review data reliability assessments, corrective actions, and data samples from training. Engage data stakeholders (e.g., IT leaders, legal experts, ethicists) to explore the data quality and reliability.[8] AI models require datasets that reflect the real world, so as a component of data audits, investigate the degree to which datasets are balanced, unbiased, applicable, and complete.

Monitor Reliability Over Time

Reliability evolves throughout the AI lifecycle. When the model output or prediction diverges from what is expected, catalogue the data for analysis and investigation. The types of data often used in this analysis are time-to-event (how long until the model diverged), degradation data (information surrounding how the model degrades), and recurrent events data (errors that occur more than once).[9]

Uncertainty Estimates

Insight breeds confidence. To give deeper visibility into how AI is functioning, there are tools emerging that permit the model to report the degree of uncertainty alongside a prediction or output. This moves toward trust in robust systems. If a model reports high uncertainty, that is valuable insight for the human operator or another networked AI. Uncertainty estimates can flag a drifting model, highlight changes in data, or provide awareness that an adversarial example entered the data stream.

Managing Drift

Operators can assess drift by comparing the model's inputs and outputs during live deployment with inputs and outputs in a reference set. Similarity is measured on a pairwise basis between test and training data inputs, with a segmentation carried out on the outputs. By maintaining a close understanding of how inputs and outputs are changing relative to the reference set, human operators are positioned to take corrective steps (e.g., retrain the model).

Continuous Learning

Establish continuous learning workflows to monitor model performance against predefined acceptable thresholds. These thresholds might include measures of how resilient the system accuracy remains in the face of small perturbations, as well as safety constraints for the system and the environment in which it is operating. As a part of this, maintain a data version control framework to enable auditability, transparency, and reproducibility of the AI model.

Ongoing Testing

Develop a testing regime that includes variability (e.g., changes in the system or training data) to evaluate if AI is robust enough to function as intended. The frequency at which models are checked for robustness and accuracy should depend on the priority of the model and how often the model is updated. High-risk, regularly updated models might best be checked daily (with a human verifying outputs). Slower changing, low-priority models could be checked on a longer timeline, in some cases using an API for automatic assessments of functionality. The results of these checks should prompt investigation and resolution of any exceptions, discrepancies, and unintended outcomes.

Explore Alternative Approaches

Given that robustness and generalizability are areas of active research, new tools, designs, and tactics will continue to emerge and advance the field. These are likely to be technical approaches, and the organization's data science professionals are positioned to explore how new ideas can support deployed AI, as well as model development. For example, "Lipschitz constrained models" have bounded derivatives that can help neural networks become more robust against adversarial examples.[10] Most simply, they promote and can certify that small perturbations in input lead only to small changes in output.

Driving Toward Robust and Reliable Tools

After digging through the training data with her team, Mariam found the cause of the calibration problems in Vietnam. It was the last thing she expected, and evidently no one else expected it, either. The dataset did not sufficiently weight how excess water vapor in the ambient air impacted calibration. It was so slight as to go unnoticed during testing, but in the real world, the ramifications were significant.

With her understanding of the issue, the AI system was removed and retraining commenced. Production in the foreign plants slowed modestly as human talent took up the task of calibrating machines. Customers received their orders according to specification and the complaints dwindled to nearly nothing. It was a hard lesson learned for BAM Inc. Even with all their attention to detail, it took just one underrepresented factor to turn powerful AI into a brittle, unusable tool.

The success of traditional software has led to an expectation that any technological tool can function as intended indefinitely and without much attention. As organizations seek to purchase or build valuable cognitive tools, they should weigh how robust the models might be in use, the degree to which their functionality can be transferred between tasks, and the resources needed to monitor and manage the tool over time.

The challenge of ensuring robustness and reliability becomes that much more important as myriad tools are deployed at scale and with significant potential consequences. Brittle AI can hamper operations, lead to poor interactions, feed bad data back into enterprise systems, and ultimately fail in delivering the value for which it was deployed.

The insight for organizations is that for AI to be trusted, it must be robust and reliable in real-world situations throughout the AI lifecycle. We need confidence that all the potential scenarios a model might encounter are considered for their impact on model accuracy, with mitigation tactics baked into the design, operation, and management.

Mathematical science shows what is. It is the language of unseen relations between things. But to use and apply that language, we must be able fully to appreciate, to feel, to seize the unseen, the unconscious.

– Ada Lovelace

Chapter 4
Transparent

Walter was the manager of BAM Inc.'s largest and most productive plant, based in Wichita, Kansas. He was a no-nonsense leader who was prized for making the right decisions that kept employees safe, production flowing, and constraints managed. He was so good at it, in fact, that when the chief of operations informed him they would be deploying a new AI system to monitor equipment function, he said he didn't need it. After all, what could a machine do that he and his team could not? His plant was the gem in BAM Inc.'s global footprint.

Despite his refusal, the system was deployed anyway and soon Walter was seeing new data points and notices flagging issues that required attention. Some of the notifications proved to be almost spooky in their predictive capabilities. In one case, the yaw of a large secondary internal motor in a lathe was barely outside of its safe operating parameters, but it could have become a problem left unattended. But other notifications were just wrong, alerting on problems that simply did not exist.

Walter did not know much about AI, and aside from a three-page memo from the corporate office, he had no idea how the new system functioned. And because of that and its inconsistencies, he did not trust it.

So when a notification told him a gear shaper machine would suffer a catastrophic failure within a few hours, he ignored it. It couldn't possibly be correct, right?

At the core of many challenges with achieving trustworthy AI is the concept of transparency, a cross-cutting feature that impacts all other aspects of ethical AI. It permits accountability, motivates explainability, reveals bias, and encourages fairness. With sufficient transparency, datasets are understood, algorithms can be traced back to their training data, and deployed solutions are understood to be accurate (or not). In this, transparency directly moves toward trust in AI.

In AI research, transparency is often conflated with explainability, but it is a broader domain. It raises questions regarding to whom and to what degree the AI lifecycle should be articulated. Do business leaders know how AI is being used in the enterprise? Are end users aware that an AI tool is somehow impacting them? Can auditors and regulators decipher how AI operates in the marketplace? Is AI transparency a component of process, and is it embedded in an organization's ethical standards and expectations?

Wrestling with these and other questions are not discrete activities but instead sit at the heart of developing and deploying trustworthy AI. Without transparency, trust in AI will be elusive, as will be the full potential value for the enterprise. Wading into this heady ethical area, we begin with a simpler question – what does it mean to be transparent?

Defining the Nature of Transparency in AI

Transparency in business practices is recognized as an important component of building trust with customers and driving business integrity. Internal transparency encourages collaboration between teams, sparking innovation while identifying inefficiencies and problems. Across the supply chain, transparency is essential not just for consumer sentiment (which increasingly weighs social responsibility as a component of purchasing decisions) but also for effective and predictive supply chain management. Transparency promotes equal treatment among employees, such as pay equality between genders, which in turn can attract more and better talent. And as it relates to laws and regulations, organizations operating on a transparent footing are positioned to adhere to the rules of the marketplace and evidence that adherence as needed.

Notice that each of those examples are areas where AI tools are being deployed. Thus, transparency throughout the organization cannot be distinct from the transparency surrounding AI.

When it comes to AI systems, transparency most simply is information about datasets, processes, uses, and outputs that are shared between stakeholders.[2] Transparency in AI is not a quality of a tool but the way in which an organization exchanges and promotes understanding of the system's components and function among different stakeholders. With this, all parties have the necessary awareness and insight into AI systems to make informed choices as the system relates to their role, be it as an executive, a manager, or a consumer. One component of this is the nature of the information shared and how intelligible it is to various stakeholders.

The OECD Policy Observatory notes that transparency requires meaningful information appropriate to the context. The goal is nurturing general understanding, ensuring stakeholders know they are interacting with AI systems, that they understand the outcome of that interaction, and are equipped to challenge an outcome that negatively affects them.[3] The European Commission uses a similar vision for transparency, noting that, particularly in cases where a user is informed they are interacting with an AI system, the information provided should be "objective, concise and easily understandable."[4]

The spirit of transparency is not just information sharing but providing stakeholders with knowledge in a way that is meaningful to their awareness and decision making. All consumers who use software or online services have encountered "Terms and Conditions" disclosures that are so lengthy and dense they often go unread. While enterprises may be legally obliged to offer this information, such an approach does not effectively promote end-user knowledge and informed decision making. True transparency in AI means genuine stakeholder understanding, and it is insufficient to place the responsibility to interpret what the shared information means on the stakeholders.[5]

For the European Commission, there are two other necessary components to transparency: traceability and explainability.[6] Traceability relates to documentation of the AI system's development, the data used to train it, the way in which it works, where it is deployed, and how versioning takes place. A robust accounting of a system from data to deployment facilitates responses to inquiries and audits. It also helps internal enterprise assessments of processes and functions, informing all internal stakeholders about the tools they are using. Explainability, meanwhile, relates to articulating how AI systems reach outputs.

Conceptualized in these ways, transparency is the conduit for promoting trust in AI. It supports legitimacy and enterprise integrity, and it leads naturally to accountability and adherence to emerging laws and regulations. Transparency in AI is centered on how stakeholders communicate and determining how best to do so. This dovetails with all other enterprise efforts to instill transparency in operations and customer engagement.

The Limits of Transparency

Total transparency, where every component of the AI lifecycle and function is shared without restriction, is neither desirable nor potentially necessary. In other domains, excessive transparency can introduce unforeseen problems; boundaries are important.[7] With AI, businesses should determine the degree to which the organization should communicate information and to whom. How much is enough? How much is too much?

Envision transparency as a spectrum. At one extreme, an organization might openly publish the algorithm itself. The Netherlands' Action Plan for Open Government 2018–2020[8] included an "Open Algorithms project," which explored making algorithms used in governance publically available. Given that the systems impact citizens, companies, and society overall, public inspection of those systems moves toward transparency, which in a democracy has real merit.

Yet, for businesses, publishing algorithms and data can disclose intellectual property. A company that invests in model development or training has an interest in limiting transparency to preserve a competitive edge. What is more, technical access to data and systems may not be particularly valuable to most stakeholders, given that most people lack the mathematical background to make sense of that information. In such instances, the better approach to transparency may be to provide intelligible explanations of how a system functions.

Within the organization, there may be no threat to IP, but different stakeholders hold varied skills and needs. Data scientists necessarily require full insight into data, processes, function, and model versions, but HR managers likely only need an understanding of system capabilities and confidence in the outputs. Finance and regulatory managers may need access to records of process and outputs to respond to audits and inquiries, but they may not need to understand the training data or how versions are managed over time. In this, the enterprise should weigh for each stakeholder the nature of transparency that is relevant for their role.

There are instances where the dimension of AI security influences the degree of transparency. When interacting with customers in the marketplace, for example, one challenge is that disclosing too much information about how an AI system operates can expose it to manipulation by bad actors. Take cybersecurity. A broadly disseminated description of how a cyber program identifies malicious activity can reveal its weaknesses and help cyber criminals devise methods for circumventing the program. Or in the insurance industry, if a criminal knows how an algorithm interprets claims when looking for instances of fraud, they may be better able to commit and conceal their illegal activity.

Meanwhile, data privacy laws and regulations are emerging, and enterprises face an obligation to guard confidential or protected personal information. If in pursuit of transparency protected information or insights are disclosed, that can degrade trust in the model and the organization. Thus, there is a tension between transparency and privacy, yielding a gray area that must be carefully navigated to satisfy the interests of multiple stakeholders.

Ultimately, enterprises should be judicious in transparency, weighing the system, the use case, and the implications from revealing information. This is particularly true in cases of autonomous decision making and the balance between reliable decisions and perceived legitimacy.

Weighing the Impact on the Stakeholders

Walter was reviewing the day's output from the Wichita plant. Everything had run like clockwork, and they were on track to hit all of their targets. Finishing up some forms, Walter expected an uneventful end to the day – and a *boom* shook the windows in his office. Shouts erupted from the plant floor and Walter rushed in to find a machine belching black smoke. Two workers were limping from the disaster and Walter's deputy shouted, "Stop the line!"

The smoking machine was the same as that the AI had warned would suffer a major malfunction. Production was stopped, and employees were injured. Walter kicked himself for ignoring the notification, and as he jumped into action to start solving problems, he knew he needed a better insight into just what the AI system did, why it did, and how he could best use it. He didn't need to know everything, but he had to learn from someone at BAM Inc. who did.

Transparency is not an all-or-nothing proposition. Determining how much information to communicate hinges on factors related to the AI impact. As a primary question, does a system make high-impact decisions? This is important not just for accountability to stakeholders, such as consumers, but for understanding when a mistake is made so as to correct the system.

Consider a chatbot helping a customer troubleshoot a problem with their entertainment software. If the system makes a mistake, it is unlikely to cause a significant negative impact. The chatbot is not subject to any regulations, and the customer is unlikely to pursue an avenue of redress, if any is even available. Yet, if the customer discovers independently that they are interacting with an AI tool, they may feel tricked, which can damage their trust in the company.

Likewise, a mistake in troubleshooting could be frustrating, and the lifetime value of the customer could be diminished because they elect to purchase a competitor's product in the future. The appropriate transparency may be simply notifying the customer that they are interacting with an AI tool and offering a clear channel for feedback that can help data scientists improve the model to avoid future mistakes.

Other AI applications can yield high-impact decisions that are subject to regulations and can lead to significant consequences. Imagine a bank that uses an AI system to score an individual's risk of loan default and determine creditworthiness. In this scenario, an applicant seeks a loan, and they are denied, based in part on the AI's creditworthiness score. There are myriad reasons why AI transparency is critical in this scenario:

- The bank needs confidence that there is no intentional or latent bias in the model training data, as well as the secondary data sources used to generate the score.
- The loan officer needs to trust that the AI outputs accurate information so they can make sound decisions. If they do not trust the output, they may elect to ignore potentially vital information.
- The adverse action letter describing why the loan was denied might necessarily include the AI-generated risk score, which should be intelligible to the applicant.
- If the denial is challenged on the grounds of a protected attribute (such as race), regulators and investigators may require explanation as to how the AI system functions.

There is also a potential for an AI system to output an erroneous score because the system is updated with new versions to address model drift. If the scoring tool delivered accurate outputs previously but began making poor judgements, the bank needs insight into the versioning history such that errors can be corrected.

Looking ahead, as AI becomes easier to use for people with less technical knowledge, organizations require processes and controls to help ensure transparency despite the fact that those training and deploying AI may not fully understand how the systems work and where they can go wrong. In the pursuit of trustworthy AI, what can organizations do to promote transparency?

Put Your AI to the Test on Transparency

- What do your organization's customers and stakeholders expect in terms of transparency?
- How is your organization monitoring and complying with regulations related to data and AI transparency?
- In which use cases is transparency most important? What is the degree of transparency required and what are the differences in necessary transparency between stakeholders?
- What data is being collected? Is it current? Can individuals access their own data? Can they opt out of its use?
- What does your organization share with its customers about the data it obtains and how/if it is used?
- Do you always disclose proactively and upfront that a product is AI-driven? Where and how?
- Do your end users have a channel through which to inquire and provide feedback?

Taking Steps into Transparency

Transparency in AI is not just buried in the data but instead is emergent across the AI lifecycle. Driving toward transparency spans the component parts of the enterprise: its people, processes, and technologies. What could be characterized as leading practices are perhaps better conceived as a cross-cutting philosophy of transparency, guiding decision making and design to produce a transparent AI-fueled organization.

People

Look across the full chain of stakeholders who require some knowledge of a system, and from that, determine the necessary transparency to engender each stakeholder's trust in AI. Internal stakeholders require degrees of transparency so they can provide essential input and viewpoints that concern other ethical qualities of AI.

Take for example a customer engagement system that interacts with existing customers and records the data for use in various business applications. Those in product development may seek to have the system collect granular information to inform innovation, while those in marketing may see such data collection as potentially hazardous to consumer trust, as it could provoke concerns over privacy and data protection. These divergent business needs should be harmonized, and reaching consensus requires both stakeholders to have an understanding of how the AI tool functions, the data it uses, the way it can be made to operate, and other matters under the umbrella of transparency.

Among stakeholders, ensure that executives and higher management are aware of how the data science and technical teams are developing and training systems. Business leaders may have some awareness of projects in these departments, but they may not know precisely what is being done, how systems are being designed, and the function they are meant to fulfill.[9] Consider how much information and understanding executives need so as to align AI projects with enterprise strategy.

Externally, stakeholders include consumers, but they also can include regulators, lawmakers, journalists, contractors and vendors, and other third parties. Not every stakeholder requires an understanding of an AI system, but in planning and design, the enterprise should think through the people with a valid need to understand AI and critically, the best way to reach that understanding. The people, their work and background, and their AI literacy all impact how the enterprise approaches transparency and understanding.

Processes

Recall the EU's three components of AI transparency: communication, traceability, and explainability. Addressing each of these must be embedded in the processes surrounding the AI lifecycle. Traceability and explainability begin in AI design. After defining the degrees of transparency required for each stakeholder, develop processes for obtaining, documenting, and reporting information that can be packaged for internal and external users.

As the system moves to deployment, maintain the consistent reporting model, creating a continuous record of how the AI functions and the impact it has across a range of factors, including decisions, versions, and errors. It might also include any relevant feedback from end users. This consistent, robust set of data helps the enterprise preserve internal and external transparency as the number of AI tools expands. Some organizations deploy hundreds or even thousands of AI systems. Maintaining control over internal and external transparency requires consistent processes.

Technology

A persistent challenge in AI and machine learning is the capacity to explain how a system produces its outputs. In many cases, the breadth and complexity of data and algorithms defies simple explanations. This can be addressed through transparent model design, complementary AI systems that aid explainability, as well as other methods. The enterprise should define up front the nature of the transparency required for stakeholders, and use that as a guide for how AI systems are built, acquired, deployed, and managed.

Trust from Transparency

When Walter joined a virtual conference meeting with the leaders in data science and AI, no one was happy. The Wichita plant would run behind schedule for several days while new parts were delivered. And the data scientists were frustrated that Walter had ignored the warning delivered by the system they had designed for that purpose.

As they discussed the tool and its use, Walter learned that it was unlikely to ever deliver accurate outputs 100% of the time.

"Well then, why use it?" Walter asked.

"Isn't a 70% chance of finding a catastrophic problem before it occurs worth it?"

As he recounted the lost productivity and impact on the company's bottom line, Walter realized the tool was never meant to supplant his decision making, only supplement and inform it. It was a guide that, while imperfect, could be woven into the plant's processes to anticipate the very accident that had occurred.

Transparency engenders trust across a range of factors. It is the beating heart of ethical AI, and an essential component in capturing the full potential these systems can generate. And it will only become more important. Every aspect of business across every industry is being transformed into an AI-fueled marketplace, and as systems multiply and are embedded in every business function, a company's future potential with AI requires attention to transparency. A commitment to transparency in AI prepares the enterprise to thrive and adapt in the era of human-machine collaboration.

A complicating factor, however, is that while organizations can be transparent in how they use AI, the AI itself can be difficult to understand. How do machines deliver insights that outpace human cognition? What precisely are the algorithms doing with the data? What is happening in that black box? We must look deeper into the technology and ensure that we can do more than use it. We need to be able to explain it.

It's difficult to be rigorous about whether

a machine really "knows," "thinks," etc.,

because we're hard put to define these

things. We understand human mental

processes only slightly better than a fish

understands swimming.

– John McCarthy

Chapter 5

Explainable

When it came to marketing efforts at BAM Inc., Chief Marketing Officer Francis was an innovator. He understood the potential in customer engagement leveraging AI, and he was determined to haul his organization into the modern era of AI-powered marketing. Francis and his team went into the endeavor full of excitement while also knowing that they were treading on new ground for the enterprise.

It was a project with huge potential and few downsides that Francis could imagine. The AI system was a customer engagement tool that generated leads by engaging users across platforms with targeted marketing. The business that sold BAM Inc. the system boasted that the tool could increase lead generation by upwards of 20% and lead conversion by an impressive 15%. All it required was a steady flow of data from which the system could evolve over time to keep pace with the real-world environment.

After a few weeks of operation, the trend in lead generation and conversion was clear – and it wasn't good. The system had barely moved the needle. A few weeks after that, the ROI on AI-driven marketing efforts was actually deteriorating.

Then Francis got a call from sales. When the sales team reached out to potential customers, they heard a common refrain: *Your outreach and materials are not relevant to my industry. You don't understand my business.*

Sales asked Francis what was going wrong, but he couldn't explain it.

With AI tools used across all industries, yielding real impacts on people and society, we should be able to explain and interpret why an AI tool makes the decisions it does. Even if the output is accurate, we still should be able to understand the reasoning behind it.

The use of neural networks gives rise to the so-called "black box" machine learning problem. The process by which models are trained and their outputs returned can be opaque, in part because the machine is performing so many calculations on datasets that defy true human comprehension. From a business perspective, this creates potential risk in as much as if the leaders and data scientists do not understand why and how AI calculates the outputs it does, they are challenged to optimize for the right functions. Put another way, you can only manage what you can see. The lack of explainability also limits AI's potential value, inhibiting the development and trust in the AI tools companies deploy. As orienting questions: What does it mean for AI to be explainable and to whom is it explained?

The Components of Understanding AI Function

Human decision making can be understood through the concept of expected utility. Basing decisions on our enormous dataset of lived experience, we calculate that the more utility expected from a decision, the better it is to make that decision, with utility defined by the decision maker. For example, a person wants to see a show downtown. If they drive their own car, they may not find a place to park. If they take a taxi, parking is not an issue but the journey will be more expensive. The person weighs which option has greater value – the lack of hassle over parking or the cost saving that comes from driving their own vehicle.

To be sure, humans sometimes justify a decision after the fact. If someone wants a luxury car, for example, they may rationalize the cost by explaining that the car allows them to save money on taxis generally. We can sometimes be disingenuous with ourselves. Even in this instance, however, human decision making can be explained in understandable terms.

What about AI? Consider three relevant concepts: explainability, interpretability, and intelligibility.

Explainability in AI means it is possible to understand how an AI output was calculated, and the more explainable the system, the greater the human understanding of the AI's internal mechanics. Whether it be a data scientist, an executive, or an end-user consumer, the more explainable AI is, the better equipped the individual is to make informed choices in interacting with or applying the model.

Explainability is a cousin to interpretability, which means it is possible to understand relationships within a system. The user can understand not just how an output was reached but also why. That in turn grants greater visibility into how the model functions in a given context. Data scientist Christoph Molnar describes four models of interpretability:[2]

Global holistic model interpretability – The entire model is understandable, including the training, the data, and the learned components, such as weights and parameters. This is potentially outside the realm of what is humanly possible.

Global model interpretability, modular – Components of the entire model are understood, such as a smaller number of weights or features.

Local interpretability for one prediction – A single instance of model prediction can be explained.

Local interpretability for numerous predictions – A group of predictions can be explained either with modular global interpretability or multiple local interpretability predictions.

There is a third relevant concept: intelligibility. This refers to how well a model can be interpreted in human terms. A model's interpretability may be accessible to a data scientist but not a lay user, and usefulness of intelligibility might best be based on who is attempting to understand a model. For example, a mapping system that tells a driver the fastest route to their destination may be highly intelligible if the driver understands the system is making decisions based on distance, traffic patterns, and speed limits. Conversely, a system monitoring machine function in an industrial area may be somewhat unintelligible as it computes raw operational data in real time, far beyond the speed and capacity of the human workers.

Together, these three concepts – explainability, interpretability, and intelligibility – are the ways in which humans can understand how a model works and why it delivers the outputs it does. Since the degree to which each is necessary depends on the users, endeavors to illuminate the black box hinge on to whom model understanding is relevant and why.

The Value in Explainable AI

Fostering trust in AI means in part demystifying how it works, and the variety of stakeholders surrounding AI deployment have different needs for explainability. Data scientists may seek deep interpretability in their models to capture greater insight for improving the tool. Business leaders in HR, marketing, and other divisions may need rich explainability to decide how to use AI as a component of strategy and operation. Regulators may insist on explainability as a means for overseeing the proliferation of AI in the marketplace. And consumers may want basic intelligibility, an accessible explanation for how and why an AI system is making decisions about them and their interests.

The challenge for every enterprise leader is to determine who requires explainability in AI function, which type, and how that impacts the business. Some primary areas where AI explainability has value include:

Driving Innovation and Application

The technical development of AI models is a practice area distinct from AI application. The data scientists who build the systems are partners to the domain experts and business leaders – across a product lifecycle and business environment – who use the systems. The explainability needed in data science to understand how and why a tool works is just as important as the interpretability and intelligibility required for the nonscientists who use the technology and imagine and innovate for business benefit. The power of AI needs to be explainable, in a useful way, to the full chain of stakeholders so they can look for opportunities to extract benefit, build better products, deliver better services, assure users of trustworthy AI functionality, and cater to the customer while advancing the enterprise.

Important factors include who is seeking value from AI and whether they have mechanisms for explaining the tool in the context of their work and the value they pursue. This takes knowledge far outside the realm of data science, from back office operations to supply chain management to customer engagement and employee retention. In this era of humans working with machines, the human element is not secondary but an equal partner as businesses explore new capabilities and seek out opportunities for improvement and innovation. This is only possible if the AI tool can be explained in a way that makes sense outside of mathematics.

Improving Model Performance

AI models are trained to deliver on a set of metrics, and if the outputs deliver valuable predictions or decisions, then the model is useful and successful. However, in training for those outputs, what else might be embedded in the AI function? Could bias lurk somewhere in the data and influence outputs that at scale begin to cause issues with fairness? What about valuable edge correlations in the data that go unnoticed but could hold opportunities for innovation and new approaches in the marketplace?

Explainable AI allows data scientists to look more deeply into parameters, weights, and correlations and seek blind spots and new opportunities that together deliver improved model performance. If we can explain why a prediction is given, we can better understand relationships between data points, which fuels innovation, continuous improvement, and continuous deployment. This is particularly important in terms of value relative to investment. If an enterprise invests in model development, avoiding bias and enhancing outputs allows the organization to extract more value for the investment.

At the same time, organizations can weigh whether to purchase AI models or develop them in-house. Business leaders should understand what they are acquiring so as to make informed buying decisions. Knowing that a model delivers accurate outputs but not knowing how it exposes the organization to unknown risks can lead to potentially serious implications, such as regulatory fines and brand damage.

Encouraging Use Through Trust

If end users do not understand why an AI tool is providing the outputs that it is, they may be less likely to trust and therefore use it. In some cases, the degree of intelligibility will directly impact this trust. A highly technical, difficult-to-decipher explanation of how a system works may be valuable for a data scientist, but it is less so for nonscientists. As an example, the U.S. Defense Advanced Research Projects Agency (DARPA) funds research into techniques that facilitate explainable AI techniques "to help users understand, appropriately trust, and effectively manage the emerging generation of AI systems."[3]

If military members do not have an understanding of why an AI tool is outputting, for example, one likely enemy location over another, or an autonomous drone's target selection, they may be less likely to trust and use it. If AI tools can offer a competitive advantage over an adversary, it is in the interest of military forces to supply soldiers with trustworthy tools, and that requires explainability and intelligibility.

As another example, in the business realm, a factory floor manager may trust her intuition and experience more than an AI system because she does not understand why the AI is recommending that a machine be shut down to prevent a critical part failure. Without an intelligible explanation for why the AI is signaling that a part will fail, the manager might simply ignore it. The consequence then is that the part may indeed fail, even as the manufacturing system had the opportunity to prevent it.

Satisfying Regulatory Inquiries

Explainability has impacts on other dimensions of trustworthy AI. In some industries, for example, fairness and impartiality in quality of service and access to opportunity are highly regulated and heavily monitored, which is appropriate. In finance or healthcare, decisions that impact the consumer are subject to audits, inquiry, and even legal challenges. With that, an organization using AI to inform human decision making must have the capacity to articulate the process by which an AI system arrived at an output. Both the organization and the regulator need to be able to interpret not only how but why conclusions or predictions were made. Failure to do so could lead to judgments of infractions, which could bring costly penalties and other consequences.

If an individual applies for a loan and his creditworthiness is decided in part by insight generated through AI, the organization offering terms or refusing credit may be legally required to be able to show that the decision was made without bias. The challenge is that there can be latent bias in data, an AI system may be biased as a result, and the enterprise is exposed to liability for unequal access to, for example, a housing loan. Explainable AI not only helps data scientists identify and root out bias in the system, because they understand how it functions, but it also provides a clear accounting of why the system made its prediction or recommendation.

A complicating factor is the question of what current regulations require, notably the EU General Data Protection Regulation (GDPR). There are references in the text of the regulatory regime that suggest an individual has a "right to an explanation," although the literal reading of the text does not say as much. Instead, several articles in the GDPR point to such a right.

A 2016 paper argued that the GDPR mandates a "right to explanation" about decisions made with regard to an individual by an automated decision-making tool (i.e., an AI system).[4] Yet, this right to an "ex post explanation" is contested in another paper, which points out that the GDPR does not specify such a right.[5] This ambiguity should elicit caution, given the untested nature of this aspect of the GDPR, as well as the expected emergence of new AI regulations in multiple countries and regions. Ultimately, prudence suggests a recognition that those impacted by AI decisions may ultimately have regulatory support for contesting AI outputs.

Factors in Explainability

While driving toward explainability, there are considerations for intellectual property (IP), privacy, and security.

IP – Data and algorithms are strategic assets. An enterprise that shows full explainability to a broad audience potentially compromises its IP, in as much as competitors could reverse engineer or more easily copy a company's successful AI system. This does not absolve a business from permitting external explainability, such as to third-party auditors, but it is a factor for business strategy that should be weighed and addressed as the enterprise decides how much explainability is needed to engender trust with stakeholders.

Security – An algorithm can be susceptible to manipulation if its functionality is understood by bad actors. In hypothetical cases, bad actors who know how a model makes decisions could find ways to game the system, by, for example, obscuring specific details about themselves to gain more favorable terms for a loan.

Privacy – Some data, such as in healthcare or finance, is highly sensitive and must be guarded, whether for business benefit or because regulations require it. In promoting explainability, enterprises must be careful to ensure that releasing information about model performance does not compromise individual privacy because details or insights are exposed to audiences that should not have access.

Technical Approaches to Fostering Explainability

With his credibility on the line (and possibly his job as well), CMO Francis needed to correct BAM Inc.'s AI customer engagement system. There was something happening in the model that he could not explain. He called the vendor that supplied the tool and demanded answers; the vendor had few to offer. Francis did not understand the math underlying the system, and he turned to BAM Inc.'s data science team. Looking through the real-world outputs, they found customer sentiment steadily deteriorating and becoming more negative with each engagement. Was it the messaging, the offering, or something else entirely? Why was the AI making the decisions that it did?

The task at hand was becoming clear. Either BAM Inc. needed more tools to explain the AI, or they needed a new system. And Francis knew that if he lost the confidence and trust of the executive team after an investment he had championed, BAM Inc.'s AI adventure in marketing might be stalled, if not retired entirely.

Explainability in AI can be nurtured in two primary ways: either the model is inherently explainable because of how it is constructed, or other tools are used to explain an opaque model. Yet, this is not a one-or-the-other proposition but instead a spectrum of possible approaches. It is up to the organization and data scientists to determine the impact on the end users, the level of explainability needed (if any), and the combination of approaches that deliver the highest explainability with the highest model accuracy.

Prioritizing Explainability

There are some instances where explainability is a low priority, such as when there is no consequence for error. For example, an online shopper may be shown recommendations for products based on previous purchases. An incorrect recommendation causes minimal harm. Explainability may be valuable for a marketer because insight could help enhance model performance and drive more sales, but ultimately, the organization and the consumer face few consequences from opaque models.

Additionally, some systems may be so well validated that explaining how outputs were reached is more academic than necessary. For example, the convolutional neural network AlexNet used for large-scale visual recognition achieved a remarkable accuracy rate in image recognition, but the quality of visual recognition systems trained on the ImageNet database has been steadily improving for years, with iterative advancements focused on reducing error rates. The core capability has long been validated, making explainability somewhat less critical for trust.

Intrinsic Explainability

Not all AI requires neural networks. Some rules-based model structures, such as linear regression and decision trees, are easier to interpret and understand. The weights, parameters, and other factors are visible and self-explanatory, allowing the organization to see how and why computations were made. The process for reaching explainability may become more complex with more numerous data and variables, but the "white box" model remains fundamentally explainable.

Post Hoc Explainability

The black box issue can be resolved after model training with post hoc methods. Explanations are reached by interrogating the outputs. Two common explainability methods are Local Interpretable Model-Agnostic Explanations (LIME) and Shapely Additive Explanations (SHAP).

The LIME algorithm can be applied to any AI model.[6] It functions by identifying a subset of variables a model uses for a prediction, and, if those variables are good indicators for a prediction, that in turn validates the trustworthiness of the model overall. As a simple example, a model analyzes data for an applicant's mortgage loan. It makes a prediction from a diversity of data points, not all of them intuitively relevant, and concludes that the applicant should not receive the loan. The LIME algorithm extracts a set of variables likely to be relevant, such as past bankruptcy, insufficient income, and significant credit card debt. Intuitively, the applicant may struggle to maintain mortgage payments and potentially default. Since the variables support the model prediction, it is possible to explain and therefore trust the model, even as all of the contributing variables may not be known.

The SHAP algorithm uses a concept from game theory to explain model predictions by calculating how much each variable contributes to the AI output. A math-intensive approach, SHAP brings together LIME and the cooperative game theory concept of Shapley Values to determine the local accuracy of a prediction, missing features, and consistency in outputs. Together, it helps explain and validate a model's prediction.

There are other post hoc explainability mechanisms, and they can sometimes be used in conjunction with one another. As with all aspects of ethical, trustworthy AI, however, explainability depends in part on the human stakeholders in model development and deployment.

Put Your AI to the Test on Explainability

- Is your organization using explainable models? How do you know?
- How is your organization monitoring and complying with regulations related to AI explainability?
- Can you explain what the algorithm does, and how the model makes decisions?
- What are the main contributors that influence the model output?
- Can you articulate how the data is used and how decisions are being made?
- Will end users be able to understand and trust the data and algorithms?
- If you cannot explain the model output, do you continue with the use case?

Leading Practices in Process

Explainability methods and the deployment of AI generally can trend toward technocentric application and interrogation. Post hoc explainability methods involve complicated mathematics largely inaccessible to all but the data scientists. The human element must permeate every phase of the AI lifecycle, embedded in process so as to guide AI explainability in a way that is useful for stakeholders. A data scientist may be able to calculate the error rate of an algorithm and show the math that allowed them to do so, but does that offer much value to the marketer, the business strategist, or the consumer? Black box explanations may be as opaque to most stakeholders as the box itself.

Thus, the AI decision-making and development process should make room for varying perspectives and needs that fall outside of the technical elements in AI. Consider these leading practice areas as components of fostering explainability.

Engage All Stakeholders

The context in which AI is deployed directly impacts the nature of explainability. It requires domain knowledge across the industry and business to develop the most useful models that support the enterprise. In some ways, it is not just about whether the model can be explained but whether the explanation is valuable. This requires not just the direction from leadership but the needs and priorities identified by stakeholders who will engage with AI throughout its lifecycle. AI must be usable, and that requires explanation of how it functions and the insights or predictions it is generating, tailored to the individual encountering the system.

As a part of this, look at the expectations for explainability resulting from existing or emerging regulations. Engage the organization's compliance and legal teams to help build explainability into a model during development, or alternatively, apply the appropriate post hoc mechanisms after model training.

Tailor Explanations and Reporting to the Stakeholder

Each stakeholder requires different levels of explanation for AI function. While business leaders require an intelligible global model showing how the system aligns with business strategy, regulators will require explanations relevant to protected attributes and equal access to services and opportunities, and consumers are most likely concerned with how an AI system reached decisions concerning them specifically.

Embed reporting controls throughout the AI lifecycle, and develop processes to obtain, document, and report the information. As a part of this, determine which information is relevant for internal and external parties, and develop standard reporting that presents explanations that are consumable for the stakeholder. This will be challenging as there is not yet much research on how people use AI explanations.[7] As with other aspects of AI, the need for explanations calls for innovation and experimentation. For consumers, for example, one approach may be to create a scorecard that quickly identifies the relevant attributes that led to an AI output.

Ongoing Explainability Testing

Because data and inputs change over time, so too do AI models and their function. Model management takes active attention on the part of data scientists, and the enterprise should regularly review whether the stated explanations remain true. This can be built into other processes for system testing and assessment. In addition, legal and compliance professionals should monitor changes in laws and regulations to help ensure model explanations and records keep pace with third-party expectations.

Another approach may be to put test cases to human decision makers that make assessments or predictions without the aid of the AI tool. If AI and human decisions agree on an output, that is further evidence that the model is valid and it also feeds into explanations of why certain decisions are reached and how to conceptualize that process in human terms. While the model necessarily reaches conclusions in ways distinct from human thinking, the process for doing so may be comparable and in that there is an opportunity to define explainability in a more intuitive way. (Note: While this approach has merit, there is also a risk of introducing a new source of variation, a common challenge found in poor label quality in supervised learning.)

The Explainable Imperative

At BAM Inc., the sales team was reporting negative feedback on a weekly basis. Francis scouted the marketplace for post hoc systems that could explain their AI's customer engagement decisions. Mustering his courage and ready to fall on his sword, Francis spoke with other members of the executive team and laid out his conclusion: "If we cannot explain why this system is performing as it is, we cannot use it."

To his surprise, the CFO, head of sales, chief of operations, and others all seemed to agree that they should not just walk away from the AI investment because they could not explain it. Instead, most stakeholders took a valuable lesson for BAM Inc.'s other ventures into AI. Explainability is not an afterthought; it is a requirement for AI that can be trusted.

Focusing on explainability today sets the stage for the methods and standards for explaining AI in the future. This is important not just from an end-user perspective but also in terms of the enterprise. Explainability helps business stakeholders understand why AI is valuable and explore areas where novel applications can generate opportunities and drive competitiveness. Indeed, interpretable AI can fuel adoption throughout the organization and reveal new use cases that may not be evident.

AI is a complicated subject area, with systems that are difficult to understand, even for the people who design and build them. Embedding explainability in the tools and processes governing their use helps bring more stakeholders into AI application and exploration. This is an essential component of seeing AI reach its full potential. There may be instances where AI outputs leave us with more questions than answers, but so long as explainability is at the forefront of our endeavors with AI, we will be in a position to ask the right questions and uncover new insights about our autonomous partners.

To every action there is always opposed an

equal reaction.

– Isaac Newton

Chapter 6
Secure

B AM Inc. was known for taking information security seriously. The company dealt with trade secrets, proprietary information, and financial data from some of the largest companies in the world. It was because BAM Inc. was so reliably focused on information security that many customers elected to work with the enterprise. Given that, Chief Information Officer Masami was respected as a mission-critical executive who always got the job done.

On an otherwise uneventful morning, Masami received a notice from a law enforcement body that cyber criminals had begun using a new exploit to attack back office AI that reviewed and settled vendor invoices. The tool looked for potential fraud while expediting payments, allowing human employees to work on more valuable tasks. The exploit, however, could mislead the AI and trick it into revealing sensitive financial information.

Masami read through the technical details of the law enforcement notice and realized the potential for harm. If the AI could be fooled, BAM Inc.'s stellar security reputation would suffer a staining blemish. She called in her team to begin identifying where their vulnerabilities were, how to patch them up, and given the threat, whether the AI system should be used at all.

Security is a necessary and pressing issue for all AI systems. We know from experience that valuable technological systems are attractive targets for bad actors. In 2020, the monetary loss from cybercrime was nearly $1 trillion, almost double that in 2018.[2] Despite the best efforts of sophisticated cybersecurity programs, losses continue. The state of cybercrime offers a cautionary window into how the future of AI security may look.

The benefits of AI may be as significant as the consequences of its misuse or corruption. A 2018 Analytic Exchange Program report on AI risks lists some of the threats that may be on the horizon: automated social engineering attacks, technology vulnerability discovery, repurposing commercial systems for terrorism, information availability manipulation, and influence campaigns.[3]

For AI, the full picture of the security threat is not yet clear, but it is still prompting hesitancy among enterprise leaders in developing and deploying AI technologies. More than 60% of respondents to a Deloitte survey cited cybersecurity vulnerabilities in AI as a major or extreme concern, and 56% see their organization slowing adoption of AI technologies because of the risks.[4]

Our trust in powerful AI that can change every industry and unlock potential requires systems that can be secured against a variety of threats, many of which are not yet imagined, much less manifest. The path forward requires an awareness of how AI tools may become compromised, the implications from it, and plans and processes to keep security at the forefront of strategy and deployment throughout the AI lifecycle.

What Does AI Compromise Look Like?

Many business leaders understand the core elements in cybersecurity: strong access credentials, active system monitoring, and employee training for effective cyber hygiene and avoiding social engineering attacks. Those elements are insufficient for AI security due to how AI systems operate and evolve, as well as the novel attack vectors cybercriminals and bad actors are still discovering.

These are the early days of AI security. Much focus is put on basic taxonomy, classifying how security may be circumvented, and from there, deciphering how it can be mitigated. As a starting point, consider a three-axis taxonomy as conceived by researchers at the University of California, Berkeley:[5]

1. Influence – An attack can be causative (i.e., influencing the data) or exploratory (i.e., observing how AI responds to an action).
2. Security violation – The attack can yield false negatives (integrity violation) or false positives (availability violation).
3. Specificity – The attack can be focused on a specific classifier in an AI system (targeted) or directed to classifiers across a system or many systems (indiscriminate).

This helps show the multifaceted challenge of securing AI at every stage of its lifecycle. With this, the organization is obligated to think and act critically to preserve security, even when the nature of the threat is evolving and perhaps not yet devised.

AI security is one element fueling the field of adversarial machine learning (AML). As it relates to security, AML attempts to penetrate, compromise, or corrupt a system so as to learn how to remedy vulnerabilities. Generally, AML can be broken into three areas:[6]

1. *Causing the system to take an incorrect action or make an incorrect decision.*

   The adversary identifies and inserts perturbations in input data that lead the system into error. Technically, the adversary computes the derivatives of the system error to find the perturbations that yield the error they seek to elicit.[7] This could be done by feeding corrupted data to a system (either during training or as the system learns in the real world). It might also be accomplished in a physical way, such as by manipulating the real-world environment. For example, researchers have shown how strategically placed stickers on road signs can lead vision recognition systems to misidentify them.[8]

2. *Causing the system to reveal data, insights, or conclusions that it should not.*

The adversary probes the system outputs to reveal data that is otherwise protected or anonymized. In a model inversion attack, for example, an adversary uses an attack algorithm that assesses a model's confidence values and then works backwards to reveal specific information. A 2015 study that used this kind of attack as part of an experiment showed it could extract data from a facial recognition system, and it could also estimate how individuals responded to lifestyle survey questions.[9] For businesses, these kinds of attacks could reveal valuable and sensitive enterprise data, as well as potentially expose the company to legal and regulatory penalties.

3. *Causing the system to learn incorrectly.*

The adversary may exploit a vulnerability in a system or create a system with a "backdoor" that persists even when the model is retrained. This kind of AI vulnerability might arise when a pretrained model is purchased from a vendor that delivers excellent performance on the client's data but also contains a Trojan horse backdoor that could be later exploited.

With this broad understanding of how unsecured AI might be manipulated or exploited, we can look more closely at some of the attack vectors bad actors might use to compromise AI systems.

How Unsecure AI Can Be Exploited

There are a variety of tactics cybercriminals might use to make an AI system operate counter to its intended design and training. New methods will surely arise and other tactics may be more effectively defeated as tools and security engineers work to keep models ahead of the threats. To understand the threat landscape, however, consider these attack paths and how unsecure AI can yield negative outcomes for the enterprise.

Data Poisoning

The attacker injects select data samples to contaminate the training data and cause the resulting model to work in a particular way. In Direct Poisoning, the attacker injects data into training data, or even alters the learning algorithm with what is called a logic corruption attack.[10] In Indirect Poisoning, the attacker inserts data into pre-processed data, such as an open-source dataset. This is a particular challenge because a major source of training data is public datasets that include (potentially unmoderated) third-party contributions, such as Wikipedia. Attackers can intentionally and over time add malicious data to trusted datasets and through that impact how the resulting model operates.[11]

Data poisoning can also be done by manipulating deep learning systems that amend and improve their functions as they encounter real-world data. Take email spam filters. Spam filters are (in part) kept relevant through machine learning. As users flag emails as spam, the system recognizes that a certain email with given words, senders, and other attributes is spam and sets a global rule, thereby sending all emails of that kind to any user into the spam folder. However, spammers can attempt to skew the system by sending millions of emails that poison the dataset that the system uses to adjust itself (i.e., the emails and user reports). This kind of causative attack can lead the spam filter to adjust in a way that creates an opening for spammers to bypass the system.

Transfer Learning Attack

Pretrained models can be used for a variety of applications, and for the enterprise, this is an expedient and cost-effective approach to deploying AI at scale. With transfer learning, a robust model trained on a wealth of data is rededicated to an unrelated task where less data is available for training. Using this approach, data scientists attempt to transfer as much learning as possible from one task to another, limiting the amount of training that must be conducted to fit the model to the new task. This saves time and resources and requires less data.

Security vulnerabilities arise when the retasked model is broadly used. Just as pieces of software can have flaws that can be hacked on any machine, pretrained AI models can have vulnerabilities that attackers can exploit once the system is fitted to a new task and deployed. There is another potential threat in this – a malicious model designer might intentionally create a backdoor that survives retraining. The model would operate effectively for the intended purpose but with a hidden fatal flaw that can be exploited at some future point.

Reverse Engineering the Code

A bank vault lock is a complex mechanism that is secure in part because it obscures how it works. But if a bank robber understands how the lock operates, they can devise methods to bypass it. So too with AI. If bad actors understand how an AI model operates, they can identify vulnerabilities and methods for exploiting it. This might be achieved by observing model outputs and inferring how they were reached, such as by building a shadow model and adjusting it until it mimics the deployed model. But it might also be achieved by reviewing open source code and any information the model divulges in its operation.

With knowledge of how the model works, attackers can devise ways to elude, confuse, or manipulate it. An AI used to detect malware, for example, might be tricked into whitelisting a program that would otherwise be identified as malicious and flagged for inspection or quarantine in a network. Likewise, fraud detection and anti–money laundering tools are subject to risk, in as much as if the algorithm is understood by a bad actor, they are better able to avoid it. Overall, attacking the model is not the end goal but instead a step in accessing other vital data or systems.

Exploiting System Errors

AI models can contain inherent biases or errors in design that create vulnerabilities. These may be inconsequential for completing the task for which the model is trained, but if they are known by a bad actor, they could be exploited to nefarious ends. These may be among the most challenging vulnerabilities because you can only fix problems you know exist.

From this overview, the threat landscape becomes clearer. There are a number of attack vectors that adversaries can exploit to manipulate AI. Enterprises are challenged to secure AI throughout its lifecycle against sophisticated attacks originating from a range of bad actors, from low-resourced individual hackers to well-funded nation states. Their reasons for attacking may be as varied as the paths of attack, but the consequences for the enterprise fall into some common areas.

The Consequences from Compromised AI

Chief Information Officer Masami led her team through a rigorous forensic review of a sample of recent vendor payments. They looked for the vulnerabilities the law enforcement bulletin had flagged and pored through invoices, wire transfers, potentially problematic companies. By their review, they found no compromise and the information security experts were pleased that their system had withstood any attack that might have already come their way.

Masami was not so easily pacified. Just because they were not yet victims of cybercriminals, that didn't mean they were sufficiently secure. This was in part because some of the payments reviewed concerned foreign companies and individuals, including the European Union and Brazil, both of which had strict data privacy and security regulations that, if violated, could cost BAM Inc. millions of dollars in fines, up to 2% of the company's worldwide annual revenue.

In terms of fines, reputation, and other harms, the consequences of an attack would be profound for BAM Inc. Masami redoubled her efforts and engaged law enforcement stakeholders. She had learned essential lessons from cybersecurity. There were two kinds of enterprises: those that had already been attacked and those that would be eventually.

Across every industry, as more aspects of any enterprise use and become reliant on AI, they will likely become increasingly attractive targets for cybercriminals. Some of the reasons bad actors may target a system include:

Data Exposure

Training datasets can often include sensitive, proprietary data. They may also contain personally identifiable information (PII), the protection of which is mandated under laws and regulatory regimes. Data protection is a longstanding concern in cybersecurity, but even if that data is well guarded and anonymized, criminals may still be able to expose or infer it by attacking the AI itself. For the enterprise, data exposure can give up valuable confidential information or harm business reputation because PII is divulged.

Loss of Intellectual Property

Developing a model is expensive and time consuming, and a compromised model can be stolen or replicated. It is often easier to train a model from the outputs of another trained model, rather than training on raw data. An unethical data scientist can reverse engineer a model by submitting large amounts of data to the model, capturing the results, and training a model on those outputs. These tactics allow a bad actor to leapfrog over the costly process of creating a model and either redeploy it for their own enterprise purposes or sell it to a competing organization. What is more, there may be system details or data within the model that reveal other valuable enterprise IP.

Bypassing Filters

If AI is used to screen content or listings, attackers can devise methods for bypassing filters. This could lead to offensive or illegal content or product promotion that yields significant consequences in terms of liability and reputation damage. Likewise, security systems for blocking malicious email or other communications could be bypassed, exposing networks and employees to secondary attacks.

Liability and Regulatory Fines

Regulations on AI are proliferating. The California Privacy Rights Act (CPRA), the GDPR, and others place heavy restrictions on how consumer data is protected and used. At the time of this writing, the European Union has proposed a significant AI regulatory framework that, while not yet law, would be highly impactful in the area of AI security. Generally, if AI systems are corrupted or manipulated, it could lead to unintentional functioning and outputs and put the enterprise on the wrong side of laws and rules.

User Trust in AI

The enormous potential and excitement around AI is fueling experiments and creative thinking about the art of the possible across every industry. If at this early stage a model is compromised and there are consequences for the enterprise, it can damage trust in AI and diminish the appetite for innovation among company stakeholders. Board members and business leaders may shy away from opportunity because the risks are made real. As it's said, you only get one chance to make a first impression, and for organizations wading into the AI era, AI security is a necessary component of longer-term success and competitiveness with AI.

Put Your AI to the Test on Security

- Has your organization created new security risks by deploying AI?
- Does your organization have strategies to achieve employee awareness of AI risks?
- How is the security of collected data maintained? Who holds the responsibility for it? Do they have

the necessary tools and knowledge? Is sensitive data being anonymized?

- Is your organization's cyber infrastructure and expertise able to tackle AI-specific security risks (e.g., adversarial manipulation of AI models, reverse engineering of data)?
- Are your AI systems vulnerable to attacks? Have you thought through each of the external physical, digital, and other risks that may occur?
- Have you considered the internal risks of fraud and abuse that may corrupt your data or model?
- Are you communicating these risks to users?
- Do you have an integrated delivery and maintenance team with defined roles and appropriate security approvals?
- Based on what you know of potential security concerns, should you still go forward with the use case?

Leading Practices for Shoring-Up AI Security

The challenge of AI security compounds as organizations deploy tools at scale. Cybersecurity is always a whole-of-enterprise activity because security threats can emerge from a variety of vectors, from phishing emails and social engineering exploits to technology systems and edge computing devices. Going forward, organizations should take AI security as seriously as any other aspect of enterprise cybersecurity, and the approaches are in some ways similar. AI security can be viewed through the familiar lenses of people, processes, and technologies.

People

Data science teams may be principally interested in developing tools for application in specific use cases, but are they also factoring in the security implications of the tool, the data it uses, and how it will operate in the real world? As with other aspects of developing, training, and managing AI tools, the expertise in system architecture and security architecture may not be found in the same person. A necessary skillset of an organization's data science operation is a person or people whose task it is to provide the security considerations and track how those are impacted by AI design and deployment. Given that AI security is still an emerging area, enterprises may look to their existing cybersecurity professionals and determine whether and how they can participate in advancing AI security.

Meanwhile, all employees have a role to play in AI security, and internal and external stakeholders need to understand expectations for security principles. What these principles are, however, is a challenge for organizations to define, as there are not yet established compliance programs for AI specifically. The organization may collaborate with industry partners to share knowledge and coordinate security efforts.

Processes

An important component of AI security is embedding security decision making and monitoring throughout the AI lifecycle. It begins by determining security objectives and risks as models are being developed or when they are being acquired from a third party. Risk assessments should be grounded in understanding how the system will be used, privacy and regulatory rules that may apply, interactions with and/or reliance upon other organizations and systems, and fundamentally, just how much data is needed to train and employ the model. Indeed, one of the challenges with AI security is the volume of data that could be exposed if compromised, and organizations should continuously monitor data consumption and exposure across the AI lifecycle.

As a part of that, organizations should establish testing processes to probe system vulnerabilities and implement incremental preventative and detective controls. This goes beyond traditional IT asset management controls and is specific to the AI's underlying technology and data. This requires a baseline of AI configurations that are monitored for changes, as well as the implementation of detection and monitoring procedures.

This calls for AI security to become a part of MLOps, which is the union and automation of AI model development and operation that accelerates the entire AI lifecycle.[12] Continuous integration and continuous delivery necessarily include continuous monitoring. This provides for ongoing awareness of how the model is performing, whether it may have been compromised, rapid application of mitigation tactics, and insight if the model needs to be retrained given the changing operational environment. What is more, should an AI system become compromised and PII is revealed, security as a component of MLOps allows the enterprise to present records of proper data handling and security measures to regulators and other authorities.

Technology

Using AI systems for cybersecurity is still in its formative stages, but there is promise for AI tools to be used to automate intrusion detection. In the near term, all models should have forensic capabilities, as recommended in a study by Microsoft.[13] This supports reporting to regulators in the event of a breach, and it also creates a trail developers can use to track how a compromise occurred, such that they might prevent it from happening again. There are also necessary AI-specific changes for an organization's technology infrastructure, specifically in areas such as "authentication, separation of duty, input validation and denial of service."[14]

Another consideration is how the model is developed and acquired. Many models may be the result of open-source code amended with custom development for a given use case. How widely used is that open-source code? Are there known exploits or vulnerabilities? To what degree does the customization enhance or degrade security? These same questions are important when acquiring a model from a third party. Enterprises should discuss with the third party whether security and forensics are built into the model and whether there are additional steps needed to enhance the model's resilience and integrity.

And in all cases, data security remains paramount. If attackers gain access to training data, they can peer directly into model behavior and conceive ways to affect its operation. Cybersecurity is likely already an enterprise priority, and it is a necessary ingredient for AI security. Even if model training is conducted offline, the data may still be vulnerable, as is the regular churn of information that results from AI operation and continuous machine learning.

Securing the Future with AI

For BAM Inc. (and its competitors) AI security was relatively new terrain. Alongside day-to-day security concerns, CIO Masami kept a close eye on the potentially vulnerable AI system. She worked with the data science and AI teams to acquire other systems to monitor for threats and communicated regularly with security agencies to stay abreast of the evolving threat landscape.

As with all types of cybersecurity, Masami knew there was no finish line, no point at which security was assured and her job was done. Instead, AI security hinged in large part on preparation, awareness, and a vigilant security posture—the same qualities of a robust approach to any cybersecurity challenge. She did not know if the threat would ever become manifest, but if it did, BAM Inc. was ready for it.

Ultimately, AI security is just emerging as a practice area with dedicated tools and best practices. Yet, lessons from the dawn of the cyber age inform us that the time to work toward AI security is now, before the threats grow more complex and sophisticated. Laws and regulations will emerge in the future to encourage AI security, but we should not wait for that eventuality. For AI to be valuable it must be trusted by the enterprise, the end users, and the broader public. Without security, that trust will be elusive and the consequences as severe as they are currently unknown.

Trail blazing and taking risks in unknown territory led us among other things to the errors; the errors led us to a paradigm that leads "before the fact" to the future. Educating people how to think, do and be in terms of the paradigm becomes the next real challenge.

– Margaret H. Hamilton

Chapter 7

Safe

Chief Data Scientist Juan always enjoyed the weekly all-hands meeting with his team. It was an opportunity to look through their efforts, spitball ideas, and measure their efforts against their goals. On the whole, BAM Inc.'s data science operation was first class. Yet, as the company moved rapidly into the AI era, Juan was seeing an increasing need to build his team's capacity to deeply investigate how their AI models performed and ensure they were worth using (critically) before they were deployed.

As a leader, Juan worked to bring MLOps to their AI processes, and at their weekly meeting, he opened the floor for discussion concerning a newly acquired system that was already entering testing. The data scientists were thrilled to report the consistently high throughput a machine could achieve when run by the new system. It was just what engineering had requested, and on the face of it, they had achieved their goal.

"Is speed the only goal?" Juan asked.

"That's what this system is for," his deputy confirmed.

"Has the utility function been optimized for anything else?" he asked, knowingly.

"Why would it be?"

Juan had seen this misstep before. With so much attention placed on the technical capabilities of the systems they built, deployed, and maintained, the human factor received short shrift. Their new system needed more testing.

AI systems are complex mathematical operations that can only do what designers and operators permit them to do. AI safety is a human charge. In pursuit of new capabilities and greater efficiencies and productivity, we must ensure that the tools we use are socially acceptable in their application and innocuous in their operation. Their objectives should align with our wellbeing, consistently and throughout deployment. As cyberneticist Norbert Wiener wrote in 1960:

If we use, to achieve our purposes, a mechanical agency with whose operation we cannot efficiently interfere once we have started it, because the action is so fast and irrevocable that we have not the data to intervene before the action is complete, then we had better be quite sure that the purpose put into the machine is the purpose which we really desire and not merely a colorful imitation of it.[2]

As increasingly sophisticated AI is unleashed on high-consequence tasks, safety cannot be an afterthought. Rather, it should be baked into the design and management of the system, and the higher the stakes, the more critical safe AI becomes.

To gain a keener appreciation for where and how AI can present a threat to safety, we look to an articulation of what it means to be safe or harmful.

Understanding Safety and Harm in AI

As with many elements in AI ethics, defining precisely what ethical concepts mean is far trickier than it might seem. If we struggle to articulate what we mean by moral concepts, how much greater is the challenge to mathematically encode it or foster it within an AI tool?

What does it mean for something to be safe? Most simply, cause no harm. But what is harm? This is a murkier question. Defining harm and who is harmed often arises in reference to John Stuart Mill's Harm Principle, which posits that an individual should be free to act as they choose provided they do not cause harm to others through that action. This is philosophically relevant for AI, in as much as we want the systems we design to maximize their utility and achieve their objectives but without causing harm in the process. Yet, a "do no harm" Hippocratic Oath for AI is not easy. Creating safe AI requires (at least for now) far more than blanket rules. Some of the domains of harm in the context of AI include:

Physical Harm

AI has the potential to cause physical harm. This could be through a machine or by virtue of system failures and inaccurate outputs. Consider a case that occurred at a shopping center in Palo Alto, CA, in 2016. A security robot used at a mall was roaming the grounds, designed to alert on known criminals and other concerns. As it moved, it bumped into a 16-month-old boy, knocked him down, and ran over his foot.[3] After the collision, it kept moving as if nothing had happened.

The child was not badly hurt, but the parents were rightfully upset. A robot meant to enhance security instead threatened it, and the indifference the machine showed reveals why physical harm from AI is so unsettling. While sophisticated for narrow use cases, AI can be oblivious to consequences that fall outside of its data collection and analysis.

Psychological Harm

Many consumers do not appreciate how often they interact with AI every day. In some instances, user awareness of an AI system is inconsequential (e.g., when an email platform suggests edits and flags typos in real time). There are cases, however, where user awareness is important because of how humans engage with AI. We are hardwired to conceive of human-machine interaction in terms of human-to-human relationships. A 2020 study from researchers at the University of Kansas found that human trust in AI is related to attachment style, which plays a core role in parent-child and romantic relationships.[4] That is, humans may be predisposed to treat AI in terms of human social concepts.

In an advertising stunt, promoters of the film *Ex Machina* created a dating platform profile and connected it to a chatbot. The result was that some dating platform users thought they were interacting with a potential romantic interest – but were actually exchanging with an AI (named for one of the film's protagonists). It was a clever marketing effort, but at least one user was troubled, saying the experience "toyed with [his] emotions so hard."[5] The unwitting participant will surely recover, but one wonders to what degree his psychological wellbeing was considered when the promoters conceived the advertising ploy.

Economic Harm

Decisions or recommendations from an AI tool can influence whether someone qualifies for a mortgage, receives a job offer, or is ineligible for public benefits. For enterprises, inaccurate AI might frustrate efficiency, productivity, and cost. Take the potential for economic harm in financial transactions.

In 2019, a wealthy investor worked with an investment group to manage billions of dollars and, as a part of that, the investor placed some money into a hedge fund controlled by a supercomputer.[6] Despite the allure of high returns, the AI led to regular losses – at its worst, a $20 million loss in one day. Claiming the investment group oversold their AI, the investor sued for

$23 million. While the investment group maintains they never promised high earnings, they are nevertheless in a legal dispute over economic harm to their former client. The outcome will hold lessons for the evolving definition of responsible AI.

Environmental Harm

An AI tool operates according to objectives and, on its own, it has no capacity to weigh its objectives against things commonly known to humans. For example, reducing waste, pollution, and environmental impact are regular issues for every enterprise, but unless an AI tool is encoded to weigh these tangential business priorities, it will pursue its objectives without regard for them.

What is more, the development of AI models is energy intensive. Training a single NLP model can produce as much CO_2 as 300 trans-American roundtrip flights, or five times the total lifetime emissions of an American car, according to a study by researchers at the University of Massachusetts, Amherst.[7] The most significant energy consumption comes during fine-tuning for model accuracy, which raises a question for organizations: How accurate does a model need to be for it to achieve its objectives? Is there a balance between algorithmic accuracy and energy efficiency?

Legal Harm

The way AI is designed and used could run afoul of a variety of laws: data security, privacy, nondiscrimination, as well as public safety. If in the course of its application a law is violated, it exposes the operator to liability and legal repercussions. This shows the cascading nature of AI harm. If an AI system inadvertently reveals protected information, it can cause harm in that action and as a result create legal harm for the enterprise. An important question for any AI system is, is this safe to use, and if so, how is it known that it is safe? What guardrails, checks, and processes can ensure it does not expose the business to legal harm, and if those guardrails fail, who is responsible?

Optimizing for Human Values

One challenge for data scientists working with AI is ensuring that the goal of their efforts is the same as the objective an AI optimizes for. In an ancient Greek story, Eos and Tithonus are lovers, and Eos asks Zeus to grant Tithonus immortality, which he does. However, Eos forgot to also ask for eternal youth, and Tithonus grew eternally tired and weak. Eos' goal in her request was not what was reflected in what she received.

On the face of it, safe AI might seem as simple as writing a universal code that frames and constrains the system. This was explored in Isaac Asimov's 1942 short story *Runaround*, where he introduced the famous Three Laws of Robotics. They are:

1. A robot may not injure a human or allow a human to be injured.
2. A robot must follow human orders except when they conflict with Law 1.
3. A robot must protect its own existence except when it conflicts with Laws 1 and 2.

In reality, the challenge for AI safety is not so simple as encoding. AI does not know what a human is, much less harm, degrees of harm, and the moral tradeoff between an action and potentially negative consequences. AI is, after all, just a series of complex equations that optimize toward utility and reward.

As Norbert Wiener said, we need to be sure that the purpose an AI is designed to fulfill is the purpose we desire, and that means aligning the AI utility function with human values. This is the so-called Value Alignment Problem, described by leading AI experts, such as Stuart Russell.[8]

Human values, generally, are how people desire things to be. For Russell, AI exists to make high-quality decisions that move toward desirable outcomes. An AI developer identifies the desire and the AI optimizes in furtherance of it. But like Eos and her request of Zeus, is the AI developer certain they have encoded for immortality *as well as* eternal youth? Will the AI optimize as desired? This leads to two problems, in Russell's view:

1. *The utility function may not be aligned with human values.* Human values are inconsistent across individuals and groups, and they are in any case challenging to define and even more so to mathematically represent.
2. *An intelligent system will act toward its continued existence and acquire resources as needed so as to achieve its objective.* The AI does not act for "itself"; it is incentivized to pursue its objective. In the longer term and with increasingly sophisticated machines, this poses a risk of unintended harm.

These questions about value alignment inspire a reimagining of how AI research is conducted and how AI systems are deployed and managed. As Russell put it, "We need to build intelligence that is *provably* aligned with human values."

Aligning Human Values and AI Objectives

Chief Data Scientist Juan instructed his team to test their throughput system in a virtual environment. They modeled where human employees worked relative to the machine and brought in datasets of accident reports, both internally and from third parties. Sure enough, the system was the fastest of any on the market that Juan was aware of. It would make a substantial impact on manufacturing flows and production.

But alongside the benefits modeled in the virtual space, there was always a persistent statistical chance that one human employee would be fatally wounded. It was not a large chance, but it was there in the data.

"Not good enough," Juan told his team. "The odds that someone is killed because of this system must be zero. We need to retrain and this time, optimize for something more than just speed."

This scenario can play out in any company using AI. If a system optimizes for one objective, other human objectives may be discounted, leading to outcomes that run counter to the design intention. A system trained to detect cancer and propose treatment may be highly effective in that narrow task, but if the patient has a comorbid ailment that the AI system does not factor in, it may fail to recommend the best treatments that move toward the true objective, which is overall patient health.

In addition to values that can be effectively encoded during design, what may be needed is the capacity for the system to learn based on operation and measures of its reward function. Rather than bracket the system within a mathematical framework, it is exposed to environmental feedback by which it tailors its operation. The method for this approach is a type of machine learning called reinforcement learning. Distinct from supervised and unsupervised learning, reinforcement learning is the AI system learning to achieve reward through trial and error. The AI operates with an uncertain utility. It learns utility and the behavior that satisfies it by maximizing the reward function.[9] Over time, the system is tuned to function in pursuit of an uncertain objective. Put another way, the system learns what humans want, rather than being told.

Reinforcement learning is largely conducted via simulators, and more effective training may be in a real-world environment, where circumstances are in flux and human values are more complicated than static datasets. Yet, learning after deployment has implications for safety. The question becomes, how much safety risk is palatable to the organization deploying AI, as well as to stakeholders? Where is the line drawn and who draws it?

The lifetime odds of dying in a motor vehicle accident in the United States are 1 in 107, according to the National Safety Council.[10] If autonomous vehicles can reliably operate with the odds of a fatal accident being 1 in 10,000, is that sufficiently safe? Is safety an absolute idea, or are we comfortable with just being *safer* than we might be without AI? If the latter, how much safety do we need, how do we measure it, and how do the other dimensions of trustworthy AI impact our understanding of safety? For example, if we cannot explain how an AI tool calculates outcomes, are we then unable to determine safety? Might we not trust AI to be safe, even if it is? These kinds of questions show the complex patchwork of concepts that together constitute trustworthy AI.

Ultimately, however, degrees of safety may not be the best lens. Perhaps safety is not a single measure but instead a suite of ongoing activities and processes that touch every part of the AI lifecycle and all of the stakeholders in it.[11]

Put Your AI to the Test on Safety

- Could the model cause harm to users, organizations, or environments? How is this assessed and monitored? Who is responsible for conducting the assessments and how often are they performed?
- Do you have the right diversity of thought and expertise to consider all possible safety issues?
- Does your workforce have the knowledge and skills to watch for and report safety concerns? Are there channels in place for end-user feedback on safety?
- Are there processes in place for regular assessments of AI safety and any potential risks that could emerge?

(continued)

(continued)

- Are you communicating the safety risks to users and stakeholders? Are there feedback mechanisms that allow the user to opt out if safety is a concern?
- Based on what we know of the possible safety concerns, should we move forward with this use case?

Technical Safety Leading Practices

There are three broad areas of technical AI safety, as identified by DeepMind Safety Research: specification, robustness, and assurance.[12]

Specification refers to defining the AI objective and ensuring that what is intended is what results. This can be broken into ideal specification (an ideal system that perfectly pursues a human objective), design specification (the real blueprint used to build the system), and the revealed specification (a description of what happened in an operating environment).

Robustness speaks to a system's capacity to function safely amid any operating conditions. The design lab is a consequence-free environment, whereas the real world is unpredictable and full of unforeseen perturbations. The system requires the capacity to avoid risks, recover from disruption, or fail in a predictable way.

Assurance means tracking and amending the system after deployment. This comes from ongoing monitoring from a variety of stakeholders and systems, such as end-user feedback, AI systems managers, and business leaders tracking AI value against strategic goals. Assurance also requires enforcement, such as with methods to better control the system when its revealed specification runs wide of the ideal operation.

As well as helping structure risk mitigation approaches, these broad categories also suggest a broader imperative for AI safety – it is an attribute that must be observed, tracked, improved, and tended from design through retirement. It requires participation from people outside the data science field. While scientists can identify the technical means for adjusting, constraining, and improving AI safety, there should also be input from business stakeholders, end users, ethicists, and even philosophers. In this new AI landscape, no one group holds all the answers, and when it comes to something as mission-critical as safety, the AI system design and management are necessarily an all-hands effort.

Bryant Walker Smith wrote that AI safety "encompasses corporate governance, design philosophy, hiring and supervision, evaluation and integration of standards, monitoring and updating, communication and disclosure, and planning for eventual obsolescence."[13] In short, every stakeholder has a role to play and facilitating that cascades into business decisions and processes. Some of the leading practices that can move an organization toward building and using safe AI include:

Set Safety Metrics for Assessment

AI systems serve different functions and carry varying levels of safety risk. A chatbot fielding customer service questions is unlikely to require regular and robust monitoring. An autonomous package delivery drone, meanwhile, carries numerous, substantial safety risks. Even during the design phase, consider which metrics will be necessary to evaluate AI safety.

Perform Monitoring and Assessments

AI safety is not a one-time calculation. Just as data scientists and AI managers monitor and correct for model drift after deployment, multiple stakeholders should be engaged in evaluating and addressing AI safety concerns through every phase of development and deployment. Safety assessments should be conducted at each phase to track how well the envisioned AI tracks with the real-world system.[14] What is more, as data and circumstances in the operational environment change over time, monitor whether the system remains safe or if new vulnerabilities or concerns are being introduced by an unpredictable environment. The organization might best log these assessments across the workflow to create a running catalogue for review and ongoing assessment.[15]

Bring Everyone to the Table

The sum of all safety issues that could arise in various environments are unlikely to be known or imagined by just one person. Many AI safety considerations still exist in the realm of the hypothetical. With a goal to build toward a real-world environment, the organization should structure processes for soliciting ideas, input, and concerns from all stakeholders, to include: AI specialists, business leaders, business unit heads, risk and security professionals, sales and customer service employees, ethicists, legal and regulatory experts, academics, policymakers, and not least, end users. When these stakeholders are given the opportunity to voice concerns and ideas, the team of individuals surrounding AI development and deployment are armed with greater awareness and insight for designing and monitoring safe AI.

Understand the Values of the Business and the End User

As a component of soliciting input from stakeholders and aligning AI objectives, integrate the values that the business and end user prize as paramount. Identify the common expectations, harmonize those with enterprise strategy, and use that insight to inform AI system development and management.

Build and Deploy for the Future

The organizations developing AI tools are vanguard leaders in AI. What is built, tested, proven, and improved upon sets the stage and standards for what comes next. Looking to the early days of the Internet, there are striking examples where, if we had been more appreciative of safety and security considerations, the Internet as we know it might be a safer place for technology and people. That is no slight against the innovators but instead a cautionary lesson: what is done today may perpetuate indefinitely, with increasingly costly consequences.

Seeking a Safer Future with AI

At the next all-hands meeting for the data science team, Juan asked how the retraining was coming along. They were nowhere near ready to deploy. The statistical chance of harming a human was being reduced, but it still was not zero.

"I'm getting calls from engineering almost every day," he told them. "They are over-eager for this to work. But they can wait. Unless we know this AI is safe, we're not putting it anywhere near our workforce. It is our responsibility to think about people, as well as data and AI."

As AI becomes an increasingly prevalent component of our modern economy and society, it is in our immediate interest (and that of our clients, customers, and colleagues) to address the safety implications from AI. Few serious scholars and practitioners fret a near future of Terminators and *2001 Space Odyssey* HALs, but AI leaders caution that safety is a factor and must be built into the systems we are creating. This should not spark fear and concern but instead underscore the type of technology with which we contend. It is game-changing, revolutionary technology that demands our close attention as it pertains to our own wellbeing and values.

If we get it wrong, science fiction has a wonderful reading list to haunt our nightmares. But if we engrain in AI today the principles of safety and an alignment with human values, we help position this technological revolution to reach its fullest potential.

The future cannot be predicted, but futures

can be invented.

– Dennis Gabor

Chapter 8
Privacy

B AM Inc.'s Chief Data Officer Marguerite could not have been more frustrated. Aftermarket product data flows should not have been diverting her attention. Nevertheless, she was almost blind to how products were functioning in a particular country whose domestic laws placed heavy restrictions on how data could be shared and exported beyond the national borders.

From her perspective, the laws made no sense. Their products featured edge computing capabilities feeding highly detailed data into a data lake where several AI systems could monitor function in almost real time. In terms of product viability and durability, BAM Inc.'s customers were getting frequent notices on how to maintain their products and potentially replace them when the time came. It was a mark of quality.

But due to domestic privacy rules, that one country just would not release the data she needed to maintain BAM Inc.'s quality standards (to say nothing of improving future products). She could not afford to ignore the problem, but the path forward was unclear.

When it comes to privacy in AI, laws and regulations are the result of where human stakeholders place ethical value, be they government bodies, consumers, or others. These can be divergent across geographies, and every company using AI must contend with the patchwork of privacy requirements wherever they operate.

The issue of privacy is most visceral when it comes to data about people. Humans create troves of data points that reflect their interests and behaviors. From the media we consume to our purchasing choices to our vital signs monitored by wearable devices, we are data generators, and all of that information is necessary for developing and improving AI tools. In some instances, the AI systems fueled by our data offer innocuous services that we find valuable, such as recommendation algorithms or updated driving directions to avoid heavy traffic.

Yet, we also create sensitive personal information through our daily interactions with technology. Medical records, personally identifiable information, financial transactions, and more fall under the umbrella of data we would hope is kept private and treated with sensitivity. Who holds our data? Are we aware of the scope of the data we have created and where it resides? Do we have any meaningful control over our data? Should we?

In AI, privacy is a nebulous factor. Like many ethical concepts, it has varying definitions and sprawling implications for AI development and use, and while most would agree that privacy is valuable, fewer have a clear sense of what privacy is and how to ensure it. Privacy in AI relates to guarding sensitive information, gaining consent for use of that data, ensuring models are resilient and do not leak or divulge protected data, using models in a way that respects privacy, and meeting the emerging laws and regulations around the world that do not just encourage but indeed mandate privacy.

For enterprises integrating AI systems throughout their operations, this raises essential factors for building trustworthy tools. Businesses should understand what data is being collected and whether customers and others have consented to its collection and use. They should create opportunities for consumers to opt in for data sharing and also voice concerns over data privacy. And if personal data is collected, the organization needs the capacity to obscure or hide the most sensitive information and have processes in place to discard it as appropriate to prevent unanticipated use in the future.

There are pressing matters for the nexus between AI, data, and privacy, but perhaps unsurprisingly, ethical questions around technology and privacy are nothing new.

Consent, Control, Access, and Privacy

The convergence of new technology, growing industry, and privacy concerns is longstanding. Samuel Warren and Louis Brandeis wrote in the *Harvard Law Review* in 1890:

Instantaneous photographs and newspaper enterprise have invaded the sacred precincts of private and domestic life; and numerous mechanical devices threaten to make good the prediction that "what is whispered in the closet shall be proclaimed from the house-tops."[2]

Their concern was prescient, as more than a century later, we post photos and details about ourselves on platforms for inspection by friends and strangers, a manicured representation of the personal life willingly proclaimed from social media rooftops. What could not have been imagined is how data shared in the public square can create cascading and problematic implications for personal privacy and data control.

There is a tension between technological capabilities, our desire to communicate with others, the data collection and AI development that happens behind the scenes, and the enduring ethical concept of what nineteenth-century Justice Thomas Cooley dubbed a "right to be let alone."

On the face of it, privacy might appear to be a straightforward matter. In the United States, for example, a 1967 Supreme Court case considered privacy as it relates to the Fourth Amendment, which protects citizens from searches and seizures without a warrant.[3] The case led to what is called the Reasonable Expectation of Privacy Test, which has two components:

1. The individual has an expectation of privacy.
2. That expectation is recognized as reasonable by society.

When these two aspects of the test are satisfied, the individual has a valid expectation of privacy and violations of this expectation are also violations of the Fourth Amendment. This is a good starting point for exploring privacy as a concept, the foundation being that privacy is something we subjectively expect and those around us view the expectation as reasonable.

However, the translation of this view of privacy to the field of AI is not so neat. Not only does the Fourth Amendment apply narrowly to restricting government action, much of the data that fuels AI was either collected with consent or blindly divulged in the digital trails we leave when using connected devices and systems. At the least, this somewhat diminishes a valid expectation of privacy as defined by the U.S. Supreme Court.

Thus, privacy in AI often points to how data is used after we have consented to its use or deposited it freely as a byproduct of our digital lives. Privacy means in part that we want some control over our information after someone else already has it, and we want a say in who can have access to that data and how it is used.

But can we control our data in this way? Can we have our cake and eat it, too? Computer ethicist James Moor and philosopher Herman Tavani suggest control is an important factor in privacy but that the notion of control needs to be amended to the reality of the modern technology landscape. They write:

> If privacy depends by definition on our individual control, we simply don't have significant privacy and never will in a computerized world. On the contrary, it seems more reasonable to maintain that sensitive personal information ought to be private even if its owner is not in a position to control it.[4]

The challenge of individual control over personal data becomes that much more intractable when the myriad data points we generate are grouped into enormous datasets that include other people's data as well. What personal control can exist in such a dataset? Individual control over personal data becomes impossible when an AI tool acts on group classifications, derives insights that have been accurately inferred but not acquired with consent, or when personal data is deduced via information that others in a social group have consented to share.[5]

Ultimately, the ethical debate over creating and using AI that is respectful of privacy comes down to data control and access such that use of the data does not create harm to the individual. Generally, we protect ourselves from potential harms (known and unknown) by keeping aspects of our personal lives private. Harm could arise through unfair treatment, manipulation, embarrassment, limited access to opportunities – the list of potential harms is significant. The fear of the unknown may exceed the reality of potential harm, but it is no less a motivator for exploring how AI and data can compromise privacy.

The Friction Between AI Power and Privacy

Marguerite met with BAM Inc.'s legal team to explore their options for extracting performance data from a foreign nation.

They talked through the domestic laws, the political dynamics, and the stakeholders who might be engaged in finding a solution. She also spoke with sales teams to explore buying trends, as well as with the employees tasked with monitoring aftermarket issues.

Ultimately, BAM Inc. was left with the reality that the enterprise needed a more sophisticated plan for capturing data in a way that aligned with the foreign requirements but also satisfied the company data demands. Like so much in AI, data privacy in this case was a nuanced challenge that required a tailored approach.

As a result, Marguerite brought together the executive team and the advisors to hash out a plan. It wouldn't be perfect or easy, but it was the kind of challenge one bumps into in AI. When exploring new horizons with new technologies, the path forward is rarely a straight line.

AI tools are only as good as the data on which they are trained, tested, and managed. Rich datasets with numerous attributes and fine details yield more powerful AI systems that offer better accuracy, decision making, or insights. Data scientists and others in AI are therefore motivated to capture and use as much data as possible. For BAM Inc., aftermarket data meant more information to improve the products. But in other cases, data privacy is more personal. In these cases, companies are faced with the ethical quandary that by creating such powerful tools, they may be treading across privacy expectations. Consider the ways in which this can occur.

Unobvious Data Collection

Many products are embedded with or connected to AI. The step counter on your wrist, the refrigerator connected to the grocery store, the free online content accessed by inputting contact information, in your car, in the office, at the mall, sitting in your bedroom – we are surrounded by AI consuming every detail about us. And in many cases, this data sharing yields value in improving the devices we use and how we engage with the world.

Yet, most of us have limited awareness of this data collection, including what kinds of information are being shared. Commuting to work, does it matter that the car manufacturer is remotely recording the pitch, roll, and yaw of the engine? What if an AI tool consumes that data, infers driving habits, passes it to an insurance company, and your rates are raised? Does data sharing matter in that case, and does it violate a sense of privacy?

Predicting and Inferring Details

Deep learning works by finding patterns in data, and in some instances, those patterns may be previously unknown because they are counterintuitive or can only be uncovered with machine intelligence working across datasets that defy human comprehension. Looking at patterns, an AI may be able to infer a data point about a person even though the person did not share that information. Like an algebraic equation, if you know two variables, you can solve for the third.

Take a hypothetical dataset that includes two data points about you: your favorite ice cream flavor and your address. This dataset includes favorite flavors and addresses for 10,000 other people, but it also contains their voting records. Imagine that a deep learning algorithm discovers a pattern that people who live in your ZIP code and prefer mint chocolate ice cream are measurably more likely to vote for a conservative candidate in local elections. Since you also like that flavor, the AI may be able to identify how you will vote even though it has no specific data on your voting history. The AI infers something about you that you did not share, and it could lead to political outreach, door knocks, get-out-the-vote tactics, and other political actions. You consented to share your favorite ice cream and later your phone is ringing with political robocalls.

Biometrics and Behavior

Connected technologies are fundamental to how we navigate the world and marketplace, and, as a result, we generate enormous amounts of personal data as an artifact of our day-to-day activities. We tell machines where we want to go and how fast. We reveal what, when, and where we want to buy, and we divulge opinions across a range of topics by virtue of the media we consume and share. And increasingly, we use our faces and our voices to engage with these tools. Face and voice recognition systems are valuable for security and text-free interaction with devices.

The consequence of all this data sharing is that we inadvertently begin to create a digital twin of ourselves, even as it may be disjointed and spread across datasets held by different parties. The voice-controlled home assistants grant easy access to internet searches, shopping, music, and other media, but it means your voice is transferred to a remote server where an AI computes your request, and in some cases, the default permissions are to allow a recording of your voice to be reviewed by human employees to improve the service. If you asked your assistant for books on fast weight loss and best gifts for a summer wedding, did you mean to tell some data science team that you want to drop 15 pounds before your sibling gets married?

Traditional Technology with New Capabilities

The combination of AI, data gathering, and existing technologies creates new considerations for privacy.[6] Closed-circuit television technology has existed for decades and proliferated across the public and private sectors. We expect to see cameras at ATMs, outside stores, attached to light poles and elsewhere, and we view it as a method for monitoring current conditions or perhaps creating a record that will be erased unless it has some utility (e.g., the store was not burglarized so the CCTV recording is discarded). When you pair this existing technology infrastructure with, for example, facial recognition software, the result is a powerful combination of tools that tread on privacy issues.

Or imagine audio data from home assistants is recorded and stored on a company's servers. The customer has consented for that data to be used, but what if the data is shared with law enforcement and paired with other tools that can decipher where you are, what technologies you use, and what is occurring in your home, which you expected to be a private space?

These instances of privacy concern exemplify James Moor's conclusion that if privacy hinges on personal data control, then privacy is not possible in our networked, highly connected technology landscape. The onus for safeguarding privacy inevitably falls on the organizations consuming the data and developing and deploying the AI model.

Beyond Anonymization or Pseudonymization

Developing models that align with privacy expectations means treating the data such that certain information is obscured. If information cannot be traced to or affiliated with a specific person, then their privacy is protected, presumably. Data privacy is not new, and just a couple of decades ago, there were proven tactics for adjusting datasets to obscure sensitive information.

One tactic is pseudonymization, through which identifying information is replaced with a pseudonym. For example, the name Jane Smith is removed and replaced with a random number. The second tactic is anonymization (or de-identification). In this, a dataset is rendered k-anonymous by reducing or replacing clear attributes such that no combination of data points in the set can be traced to fewer than k individuals. The higher the value for k, the more difficult it becomes to identify a specific individual in the data by combining identifying data points.

These tactics when paired were sufficient, in the past, to guard datasets which were smaller and less granular. Today, however, datasets contain potentially hundreds of data points related to a person, everything from their shopping habits and travel routes to their media preferences and much more. Anonymizing and pseudonymizing is difficult to scale effectively in the datasets we use today.[7]

This is particularly challenging since so much training data is acquired in its raw form from open sources or third parties. These are wedded with enterprise data to create rich personas for individual customers. For AI, the implications are many. The model may infer data that introduces bias, or it may through its function reveal too much about the training set or the people it impacts after deployment. Data leakage can compromise privacy and lead to potential harm and security concerns for the individual.

As a truism, the poorer the training data, the less accurately the deployed AI system will function. In differential privacy practices, patterns in groups are shared, individual data is withheld, and noise is injected into the dataset to further obscure identifying information. However, this can have a devastating impact on AI accuracy.[8] Therefore, data scientists are on the one hand called to adjust the data to protect the sources, and on the other, they must preserve the depth of the data such that they can train models that operate accurately and predictably in a real-world environment.

One approach to mitigate potential privacy compromise in the data is known as federated learning. In this, data is not aggregated into a central dataset replete with sensitive information that must be obscured or removed. Instead, the algorithmic training is accomplished across edge devices where the data is generated. By never bringing the data together into a central repository, the sensitive information is that much more obscured.

More approaches are sure to emerge to solve the same underlying challenge: maximum data quality with minimal privacy threats. New laws and regulations are forcing the matter.

Privacy Laws and Regulations

To date, privacy laws and regulations have been largely based on the "notice and consent" model. When visiting a website, for example, users are commonly presented with a pop-up notifying them that their data will be collected. Sometimes the user has the option to opt in or out of which kinds of data are collected. A similar "notice and consent" approach is found in the Terms and Conditions of products or services, written in legalese so dense the everyday consumer is unlikely to read it.

The notice-and-consent model is decreasingly valuable today.[9] How much less appropriate will it be for treating privacy when multiple AI systems are operating in the public square? Placing the onus on the consumer to consent to their data being stored and used belies the reality that in the digital world, data control by the individual is decreasingly possible.

Alternative approaches are emerging, although bureaucracies rarely move at the speed of innovation. Still, there are some notable regulatory regimes around the world that reveal the kinds of rules that are sure to come, and enterprise leaders and their legal counsel would do well to study where world governments are headed in their rulemaking.

General Data Protection Regulation (GDPR)

The General Data Protection Regulation is a broad approach to protecting the data of European Union residents. It sets out extraterritorial jurisdiction, meaning the regulations also apply to non-EU organizations processing the data of EU residents. Chapter 3 of the GDPR is focused on "rights of the data subject," which regulators saw as distinct from data protection. The Chapter 3 articles require organizations capturing and storing data to be responsive and faithful to consumer requests, including:

- Explaining in plain language how data is processed.
- Notifying users their personal data has been collected.
- Providing an explanation for how the data is used and giving personal data to the user upon request.
- Giving users an opportunity to correct inaccurate data.
- Deleting any information about a user when requested (i.e., "the right to be forgotten").
- Honoring the user's right to restrict processing, request data be given to a third party, and object to how data is used.

One point of tension between these rules and how AI systems are trained and used is the right to be forgotten. If a user requests an enterprise to delete their data, it is no simple matter. The data may already be pseudonymized and anonymized, but more than that, once an AI system is trained, it is difficult to untrain it. The personal data might be removed from the dataset, but that does not mean the model necessarily changes. This is an example of the thorny ethical questions that do not have simple or even viable solutions, yet.

While the solutions are devised, the regulatory expectations already exist, and the financial penalties for GDPR violations can be significant. In one example, a major airline was fined EUR 204 million for a cyberattack that exposed hundreds of thousands of customer records. In another example, a popular search engine was fined EUR 50 million for failing to provide users with enough information concerning data consent.

California Consumer Privacy Act (CCPA) and California Privacy Rights Act (CPRA)

The CCPA went into effect in January 2020. It applies to for-profit organizations with $25 million or greater revenue; buying, receiving, selling, or sharing personal information of 50,000 or more consumers; and generating at least 50% of revenue from selling personal information.[10] Similar to GDPR, CCPA is focused on consumer rights to exercise control over how their data is used. The regulations include:

- Consumer right to request information on which data is collected, how it is used, and with whom it is shared.
- The right to be forgotten, with companies deleting all information on request.
- Consumer control over access to their information, including the right to opt out of having data sold to a third party.

In practice, CCPA requires affected companies to disclose the information collected, honor consumer requests, provide opt-out mechanisms including a "Do Not Sell My Personal Information" link, and opt-in consent for children's data. The right-to-be-forgotten rule presents a similar AI challenge in that removing the data does not necessarily change the AI tool that was trained on the data.

In January 2021, the CPRA went live, amending and expanding CCPA. It provides more consumer rights, puts steeper fines in place for intentional violations that involve the personal information of minors, and establishes the California Privacy Protection Agency, which enforces CPRA.

Other Notable Privacy Laws

The GDPR and CPRA are sure to influence how other nations and authorities develop similar tools for guarding consumer data privacy. Brazil's General Data Protection Law is modeled on the GDPR and contains similar consumer rights and extraterritorial jurisdiction. It also includes a provision for a consumer to request a review of decisions made about them by automated decision making (i.e., AI).

At the time of writing, several regulations and pieces of legislation around the world are being developed, debated, and unveiled, such as China's new Personal Information Protection Law, Canada's proposed Digital Charter Implementation Act, and India's Personal Data Protection Bill. A challenge for businesses going forward is to simultaneously meet existing laws while monitoring the development of new legislation and regulation in the regions where the enterprise operates.

Put Your AI to the Test on Privacy

- Does your organization know what customer data is being collected and why?
- What is the intended use of the data you are collecting? Are you making customers aware of this intent? Is the data being used in a way beyond the stated intent?
- Is it clear how and to what extent your organization is permitted to use data it has obtained? Has your organization developed appropriate protocols around the use of data (including when permission/acknowledgment is required)?
- Do your organization's customers have the required (or if not required, an appropriate) level of control over their data, including the ability to opt in or opt out of having their data shared?
- If the organization's customers have concerns about data privacy, do they have an avenue to voice those concerns?
- How does your organization identify, evaluate, and monitor compliance with data privacy rules and regulations?

Leading Practices in Data and AI Privacy

Regardless of laws and regulations, businesses have an interest in protecting consumer data and thinking through how the AI systems they deploy might impact the privacy of individuals. There is an ethical obligation but also a business motivation: if consumers do not trust how a company treats their data, they do not trust the company. In this, trustworthy AI supports consumer confidence in the enterprise.

Toward this end, there are a variety of leading practices that can be valuable in advancing practices and systems that respect and preserve privacy.

Supplementing the Datasets

AI models like generative adversarial networks (GANs) and autoencoders permit the creation of synthetic data. This is artificial data modeled on real data. It maintains the same structure and properties of real data but none of the real or specific information. In addition to supporting privacy, using synthetic data is potentially a much cheaper approach to gathering data and could vastly surpass real-world data in the years ahead.[11]

Obtain Informed Consent

Regulations mandate that consumers must have the opportunity to opt in or out of data collection, and to make that decision they require clear articulation of what data is being collected and how it will be used. The enterprise should determine the workable methods for ensuring the individual has enough information to give informed consent. This might include explaining how data will be used appropriately in AI systems. At the same time, enterprises should explore the datasets they purchase from third parties or find in open-source forums to help ensure the necessary consent has been granted at some point in the data collection process.

Define Privacy Objectives

Determine the objectives related to privacy, including what information to collect, how long information will be used, how information will be retained, how information will be used, and how information will be disposed of when it is no longer needed or a consumer exercises their "right to be forgotten."

Engage Stakeholders

Particularly given the laws emerging, enterprises should turn to their legal counsel and privacy compliance attorneys when soliciting data, setting policies, developing products and services, guarding sensitive information, and responding to consumer inquiries. Attorneys need to understand not just the law but how the data, AI, and related technologies function.

The Nexus of AI Trust and Privacy

After much discussion, planning, and coordinating with foreign stakeholders, CDO Marguerite made progress in establishing some palatable workarounds for the foreign country's strict data privacy rules. It was not perfect, but it was a step in the productive direction. Data on local servers could be curated and shared, not in real time but it was better than no data at all. In this way, Marguerite and others in the enterprise navigated this challenging area of AI and harmonized internal data demands with real-world limits on what people and governments are willing to share.

Privacy as a concept is a moving target. By the time standards and laws catch up with the technology landscape, innovation has already rendered them behind the times. Privacy impacts each person, and almost all people have aspects of their lives they want to keep private. Most people want a measure of control over how data is shared and used, and in the absence of control, they want confidence that the data will be used responsibly and to their benefit.

Yet, as shown, data control is illusive, and the pipelines of data flow fast around the world. Consumers are ill-equipped to understand how AI even works, much less play a leading role in governing how their data contributes. This leaves businesses with the responsibility to think through how best to preserve and protect privacy on behalf of the customers and partners. If we are to use AI to its greatest benefit, we need widespread trust, and that requires a focus on privacy.

144

When I consider what people generally

want in calculating, I found that it is

always a number.

– Al-Khwarizmi

Chapter 9

Accountable

As the Chief Procurement Officer, Akmal considered himself more progressive than CPOs at other companies, and he had the suite of predictive AI tools to prove it.

"There's more to procurement than managing constraints and winning in the margins," he had said to the Chief Financial Officer when making the case for the system. "We need more visibility into our supplier tiers, and we have got to be more nimble."

The CFO was somewhat less than enthusiastic at first. What was a CPO doing thinking about AI anyway? After some convincing, however, the CFO signed off on the investment and the Chief Technology Officer joined the effort to bring AI to procurement at BAM, Inc.

Several months later, Akmal sat down at his desk and turned on his computer. There were no paper documents to push around, not even a spreadsheet on his desktop. Instead, Akmal opened a procurement program that took in bills of materials, autonomously scoured the networks for availability and cost, and made recommendations for what should be purchased from whom and sent to where. All in a day's work for an AI-fueled procurement office.

Then the phone rang. It was the CFO, and he was not happy.

"Akmal, I'm looking at invoices for raw materials on the Anderson project, and we are paying nearly 15% more per ton than we were before your fancy new AI tools."

"No, that can't be right," said Akmal. "We have optimized for efficiency and timeliness, sure, but that couldn't possibly lead to such a large increase."

"Who is responsible for this?"

"I don't know, sir. I can't believe we've lost so much in margin."

"Fix it, or I'll put you in the margin."

Akmal's morning had taken an unexpected and unwelcome turn. Deflated and concerned, he set about trying to figure out who was accountable for the error and who was positioned to correct it.

Accountability is an intuitive aspect of human morality, so much so that we expect it in every context. Accountability underpins the rule of law and guides how restitution is calculated. It is a component of social trust between citizens, and a necessary component of professional activities in business and government. Throughout, because people and organizations are accountable for their actions, we make predictions about how others will act and how that might impact us.

What happens when an AI model makes a decision with a negative impact on an individual or organization? Who is accountable for that? The model itself cannot face any real consequence. It cannot make an apology; it has no anima. Instead, accountability is a uniquely human ethical priority – one we should embed in the tools we use and the systems that surround them.

The starting point for unraveling the challenges and potential solutions is a closer definition of this vital ethical concept.

Accountable for What and to Whom?

Accountability is essential for trust in people, organizations, and systems, and given its importance, it has received expansive study and debate across disciplines. The judicial system is the most obvious field concerned with accountability, but there is also managerial accountability in terms of financial management and political accountability as it relates to faithful representation of the electorate. Ultimately, there are numerous types of accountability and AI touches all of them.[2]

To break open the concept, take AI ethicist Virginia Dignum's view that accountability means the AI system is able to explain its decisions, and the decisions can be "derivable from, and explained by, the decision-making mechanisms used."[3] According to Dignum, accountability is not a discrete characteristic of a single AI tool but instead the components of a larger sociotechnical system that provides for accountability and is based on moral values and governance frameworks.

Other scholars posit that accountability is the product of acknowledging one's "answerability" for decisions and actions.[4] By this view, accountability can be seen as a feature of the AI system, a determination of individual or group responsibility (also called algorithmic accountability), and a quality of the sociotechnical system.

For our purposes, accountability means that not only can the AI system explain its decisions, the stakeholders who develop and use the system can also explain its decisions, their own decisions, and understand that they are accountable for those decisions. This is the necessary basis for human culpability in AI decisions.

Because the decisions machines make take place in the context of other social and technical systems, there is a range of stakeholders in AI application, and they are governed by a variety of laws, regulations, and social expectations. This creates an enormously complex landscape where there may be numerous individuals and entities with some accountability for AI outcomes.

In the case of Akmal, the CPO, his sudden challenge to identify the responsible parties in his AI error raised pressing questions. Who is accountable for the incident? Is it the vendor who supplied the systems? The data scientists who tuned it to BAM Inc.'s requirements? Was it Akmal and his procurement team optimizing for the wrong functions? Was it the CFO for approving the investment? Are we attempting to decide who is most accountable or everyone who is accountable?

This question of causality is incredibly dense and does not lend itself to a neat parsing of accountable parties. The challenge becomes that much greater when the AI tool's complexity increases, the consequence of its decisions magnifies, and it is deployed at scale alongside dozens or hundreds of other systems.

Part of the challenge is that while other large systems (e.g., financial, logistics) have received decades of study, investigation, legislation, and debate, AI has not yet received the same full treatment. The pace of innovation in AI is so rapid that we have constructed powerful tools that raise profound ethical questions far in advance of the development of rules and expectations for accountability. The broader sociotechnical system in which AI exists is still in its formative stages. Industry leading practices, governance frameworks, laws and regulations, declarations in terms of use – these and other features of a sociotechnical system that prizes accountability are in flux.

The result is a fuzzy consensus of who is accountable for what and to whom. Enterprises deploying AI are left to define what accountability means in the context of their policies and stakeholders. And for better or worse, they cannot wait for these things to be debated in academia and codified in law before taking action.

Balancing Innovation and Accountability

There are myriad individuals involved in developing and using AI tools, and when something unexpected occurs, a neat distribution of responsibility is unlikely. In an enterprise, AI responsibility may fall across the data science team, the business unit leaders, the frontlines sales professionals, and many others. The challenge of identifying responsibility becomes that much more problematic when deploying AI models that change over time or those that create new algorithms.

No matter the challenge, determining who is responsible is necessary to instill a real sense of accountability throughout the workforce. An advisory board is potentially well positioned to promote accountability with oversight, defined processes, and clear penalties for bad consequences from AI application. When employees (at any level of the enterprise) understand and embrace their accountability in the AI lifecycle, it can create a chain of people who collectively move toward AI that adheres to the applicable areas of trustworthy AI. It places visibility on the individual. At the end of the day, it is the human (not the AI system) who must answer for the outcomes, good or bad.

Yet, there is a tension between bold innovation that leads to more powerful solutions and an individual's accountability and responsibility. If data scientists, AI engineers, and others are overly concerned about professional ramifications from outcomes that they may be unable to predict, they may limit the scope of their efforts. However, this tension between innovation and accountability is not an either/or consideration. Accountability cannot be an afterthought in the pursuit of powerful, game-changing AI.

Thus, enterprises may be best served by not focusing on who is to blame when things go wrong but instead whom to call on to make things right. With a clear articulation of who is account-able for what and to whom, the business is prepared to respond to AI outcomes and take real accountability for addressing errors with corrective actions.

When AI stakeholders have confidence that humans under-stand their accountability, it engenders trust in the AI tool and the broader AI ecosystem. Longer term, when AI accountabil-ity is embedded throughout the organization with established and tested expectations, it promotes trust in AI generally. The standards for accountability that are established today will have a real and important impact on reaching the full potential of AI going forward.

Laws, Lawsuits, and Liability

As self-driving cars hit the road in greater numbers, the poten-tial for fatal accidents increases and that inevitably leads to calls for restitution, if not punishment. A human driver who is negli-gent and who strikes and kills a pedestrian could face civil suits or criminal charges. What of self-driving cars? There have been instances of fatal crashes with self-driving cars that have resulted in civil action.

To this point, we have considered causal accountability, that is, identifying the accountable person, their decisions and actions, and how those decisions and actions led to specific out-comes. Related but distinct from causal responsibility is legal accountability. Even as AI innovation is outpacing regulation and legislation, there are existing laws that apply to incidents of AI harm.

Most simply, AI in the eyes of the law is an artifact,[5] which means product liability laws can be used to seek restitution in instances of harm, be they to one's person or property.[6] Under tort law, which covers civil wrongs, an enterprise could be sued for things like negligence, manufacturing flaws, and a failure to warn. Under contract law, the enterprise may be found to have created either explicit or implicit warranties for the AI tool through its sale, which makes the company liable for harms that fall under the presumption of safety.

Notice that these remedies are focused on compensation, rather than a criminal judgment. Will this always satisfy the public demand for accountability under the law? One potential risk is that an unscrupulous organization may see legal settlements as just the cost of doing business.

In terms of broader business and consumer trust in AI, monetary restitution may not satisfy our human desire for retribution, leading to what legal expert John Danaher has called a "retribution gap."[7] When a human being does wrong, our moral intuition is that they should suffer some punishment because they deserve it. A reckless driver who causes a fatal accident could face criminal charges, which most legal systems around the world hold as just. AI itself cannot face any punishment at all, and we will need to contend at some point with the public's valid desire for real punishment for AI wrongs when there is no single person to punish in a meaningful way. If an enterprise pays a settlement and fires a data scientist, is that enough?

The lesson in this is not that enterprises should find people to blame but instead to recognize that legal responsibility is a significant component of the social and technical systems around AI. In some instances, financial restitution may not satisfy expectations for justice. Thus, as a part of AI strategy, development, and use, all stakeholders should appreciate the legal consequences of bad AI outcomes and take from this additional motivation to own their individual accountability.

Put Your AI to the Test on Accountability

- Do your organization's employees and customers know when they are using AI and are they familiar with (or have access to) the organization's AI policies?
- Is it clear who is ultimately accountable for AI and related outputs? Who is monitoring the AI and how frequently? Who will attend the hearings to defend the company if the AI runs afoul of rules and laws?
- How will you communicate if an AI operates outside of its function and causes a problem? Does your organization have an established protocol to follow?
- What are the consequences for the accountable parties when AI causes harm, damage, or violates regulations or laws?
- Has your organization adapted management reporting processes to help ensure that those charged with governance have sufficient visibility into the unique, dynamic risks of deploying AI systems?
- For complex AI systems that have business-critical impacts, does your organization have plans to address deficiencies in a time-sensitive manner? What is the monitoring process with respect to remediating deficiencies?

Leading Practices in Accountable AI

Returning to CPO Akmal, his quest to identify who was accountable for the AI mishap led him to startling insights. The data scientists who tuned the model readily agreed they had not optimized the system for cost because they were told to focus primarily on efficiency and timeliness. When materials costs began to rise, the procurement team was insufficiently experienced with the system to notice the growing problem. When they did notice it, they could not explain it and the issue persisted until the CFO found out.

For BAM Inc., the enterprise systems, business processes, and employee training were not connected in such a way that accountable stakeholders could see a problem coming and correct it. The AI tools were acquired and deployed, but the people and processes were not sufficiently aligned.

Using AI is a whole-of-enterprise endeavor. Not all AI tools present the same level of concern when it comes to accountability. Thus, the intended use, potential impact, and a variety of other factors shape how accountability is woven into the AI lifecycle, from conception to model retirement. For accountable AI, consider these leading practices across the familiar lenses of people, processes, and technologies.

People

Accountability applies to all AI stakeholders. There are a variety of perspectives and priorities across leadership and enterprise divisions with a stake in how AI functions, its intended value, and how ethical matters need to be weighed. What is needed is a multistakeholder group, including individuals working in legal, governance, risk, regulatory compliance, and analytics. All members should have access to end-to-end data on the model's operation.

Organizations should ensure that all stakeholders understand their specific roles and the impact of their decisions. If individuals are to be held accountable for the choices they make, they need to understand the scope of their accountability.

Organizations should find a balance between enforcement actions, which are necessary, and the freedom to innovate and experiment, which is also important. If enforcement actions are too onerous, it could lead to a chilling effect in innovation. Nevertheless, accountability requires enforcement of expectations and consequences for poor decisions.

An organization's people must not just know they are accountable for their decisions in AI but also understand how to live up to those expectations. This takes training throughout an organization. Stakeholders should be incentivized to think about AI ethics as a component of the workflow and report concerns or insights to the right decision makers in the enterprise. Toward this end, one approach is integrating AI ethics training as an extension of the integrity training many organizations already conduct.

Processes

Given the vast amounts of data needed to train AI models and operate in the real world, part of accountability is the protection of data and the forthright description of how it will be used and how long it will be stored. Organizations require policies on what information is collected, steps for obscuring or removing personally identifiable information (when appropriate), and who is accountable at different phases of the AI lifecycle for data protection and ethical use.

Organizations require clear operating structures and reporting lines to provide appropriate oversight of the organization's use of AI. Empowering people to report concerns or flag issues allows the entire human workforce to participate in ensuring the AI tools operate as intended and without additional negative outcomes.

Awareness of a problem is central to accountability. The enterprise should establish mechanisms to communicate and evaluate deficiencies or indicators of deficiencies in AI models. This should include pathways for both internal and external complaints.

Technology

The AI model and the computing infrastructure around it should have accountability baked into the design. This includes data collection and synthesis from a variety of sources on AI operation and the ability to explain how outputs were reached and the confidence levels of those outputs.

If an AI tool is acquired through or operated by a vendor, confirm that the model has been developed with attention to accountability measures.

Keep in mind that emerging laws may place legal responsibility on the enterprise operating the technology and not on the people or organizations that originally developed it. Enterprises acquiring AI tools can face the same legal consequences as if they developed the tool in house.

Accounting for Trust in AI

Accountability underpins the other concepts of trustworthy AI. If a model delivers biased outputs, someone is responsible for remedying it. If an AI tool is not secure and sensitive data is leaked, humans are at fault. Any time AI becomes untrustworthy, there is a person or people who are accountable for that outcome.

The challenge today is twofold. For organizations developing or acquiring AI tools, there is an evident need to establish the processes and internal rules that bake accountability into the entire AI lifecycle. At the same time, legislators, regulators, and other authorities will increasingly seek to ensure AI accountability through laws and mandates. Together, what may emerge is a new common understanding as it relates to emerging technology, the much discussed sociotechnical system that requires and promotes accountable AI.

No computer is ever going to ask a new,

reasonable question. It takes trained people

to do that.

– Grace Hopper

Chapter 10
Responsible

One of the reasons Elsa was such a competent Chief Operations Officer for BAM Inc. was that she always had a sense of the big picture. While departments throughout the company focused on meeting internal goals and aligning with enterprise strategy, Elsa saw BAM Inc. in the context of its history, its planned future, and how it impacted stakeholders, customers, and employees alike. For her, the persistent question was how to balance enterprise growth with ethical operations and plain good business.

While roaming the company HQ, looking for problems that needed solving, she wandered into the data science lab, where everyone was out to lunch. Elsa looked over the whiteboard covered in red and green marker. It was a list of ideas for AI systems that could be developed internally, deployed rapidly, and deliver outsized ROI. She read the list and saw a proposed chatbot to communicate with vendors, an automation system for populating various reports, and a shop-floor recognition system to monitor for safety concerns.

But at the bottom of the list was an idea that left Elsa concerned: "customer personality assessment from internet scrape (search engine, social media, etc.)"

What in the world was that? BAM Inc. had a reputation for being an honest partner, and whatever "personality assessment" and "internet scrape" meant, Elsa was fairly sure it was not in line with the company values. With questions and concerns, she went in search of the data science team.

As the field of AI has grown beyond academia into everyday commerce, there have been powerfully impactful innovations (e.g., tumor screening). As the enormous potential in AI (particularly deep learning) has become evident, there has been and still is a rush throughout the public and private sectors to grab new tools and put them to work, sometimes with insufficient attention to the long-term implications. It is the proliferation of good and bad use cases and systems that fuels the focus on ethics in AI today.

AI development is bookended by the question of responsible use. At ideation, when approaching deployment, and at identified stops in between, organizations must answer a fundamental question: Is it a responsible decision to deploy this system? The more we focus on this, the better equipped we are to cast aside systems that violate trust and enterprise values and expand our AI efforts elsewhere.

Globally, the enormous range of industries and business models, laws and regulations, customs and expectations make it impossible to create a granular list of what is and is not a responsible application of AI. Each enterprise should decide for itself whether the systems it deploys can be used in a way that does not present a chance of harm or run afoul of the company's ethical principles.

Of course, responsible decision making in the business realm is not a new concept. Digging into how we understand business responsibility opens the door to exploring what that means for AI.

Corporate Responsibility in the AI Era

In an ideal world, enterprises could implement a data scientist's version of the Hippocratic Oath to "do no harm" and that would be the only North Star for their efforts. This is not only too broad a charge (in as much as "harm" is a nebulous concept), it also does not include other enterprise priorities, such as maximizing profits and shareholder value. Ultimately, one cannot exist without the other. If AI application does lead to harm, company value could suffer, and if the only priority is profit, then responsible AI may be given just a passing notice.

There are some lessons to be taken from the popular concept of corporate social responsibility (CSR). In 1953, Howard Bowen was among the first to explore the notions of business ethics and an enterprise's responsibility to the public, society, and the country or countries where an organization operates.[2] This was later expanded upon and captured by the Committee for Economic Development with the idea of a social contract. The Committee wrote in 1971: "The interaction between protagonists of substantial reform of major institutions and a generally concerned citizenry is producing significant changes in public expectations of business."[3] It is fair to see this same interaction beginning to play out today in the realm of AI.

Businesses contribute goods and services, jobs, economic productivity, tax revenue and more – all things that are essential for a healthy society. Businesses can change the course of history with innovations that make new things possible. And revenue leads to shareholder profits, which are critical for a healthy investment ecosystem and national economy. But this is not enough. Scores of surveys and studies[4] have shown that for the Millennial generation, purchasing decisions are influenced by a company's efforts toward the social good, such as in limiting environmental impact; promoting diversity, equity, and inclusion; and sourcing sustainable materials through supply chains that respect human rights.

It is likely that as public awareness and understanding of AI and the ethics of AI deployment broaden, the notion of CSR will inevitably expand to include whether an enterprise's uses of cognitive tools support public wellbeing. In this, the way AI impacts common priorities for CSR will help bring together the notions of the social contract and responsible AI use.

As an example, by virtue of the power required, model training has a substantial carbon footprint. Training just one large AI model can result in the emission of more than 626,000 pounds of carbon dioxide equivalent, which is approximately the same as the lifetime fuel emissions of five consumer cars.[5] Today, the trend in energy requirements for model training is near exponential. In one study, the computational power required for training large AI models has been doubling every 3.4 months since 2012.[6]

This enormous energy consumption is none too salient for the average consumer thus far, but in a time when ecological concerns are dominating geopolitics and business decision making, it is reasonable to see the energy cost of AI as a component of a larger set of CSR principles. This shows how AI systems are not just novel tools developed in a lab. They can have a broader impact on the enterprise, the society in which it operates, and the sentiments of consumers and other stakeholders.

The same view can be taken of things like diversity, equity, and inclusion. Is it a responsible decision to use AI models trained on biased datasets by a demographically homogeneous data science team? If not, has the organization taken purposeful steps to clean their data of bias and build a team that reflects a diverse, pluralistic society?

Ultimately, technology is not inherently good or bad. What is important is how it is used and the value it contributes not just to the company and its shareholders but also to society.

Motivating Responsible AI Use

The impact from AI is rising every day, and looking ahead, the trend is clear. More powerful AI systems will continue to leave the lab more quickly and in greater numbers. With this, decisions of responsible AI use should not be left at the feet of a company's data science team. Expecting data scientists to be at once innovators, technologists, and ethicists is a recipe for poor AI outcomes. They need guidance and input, and ultimately, the decision to deploy a system should rest at a higher level.

Consider social media. The algorithms running beneath the surface of social media platforms are trained to a variety of functions, but one primary goal is to keep the user engaged for as long as possible. The more time a user spends on the platform, the more advertising can be served to them and the more data can be collected. There is nothing inherently concerning about optimizing for "time on page." If the business model is selling ads and data, then algorithms that move toward that end are doing precisely what the enterprise requires.

As is becoming increasingly clear across the world, however, algorithms designed only for time on page have unexpected and highly consequential outcomes. Real-world examples and ongoing research[7] show how delivering content that users may find most interesting can lead to echo chambers that magnify extreme views, inhibit nuanced discussion, and create closed communities that may be susceptible to false or misleading information. They can also open the door to online bullying, cyberstalking, and exposure to explicit content.

Should the data scientists have foreseen these outcomes? Or was it managers and business strategists who needed to weigh in? If the business model requires time on page as the most important utility function, then perhaps the enterprise itself is at fault.

The guidelines for these questions are still being developed, even as there is mounting momentum on the part of legislators and others to regulate the social media industry.

This is not just a social media concern. With scandals, congressional inquiries, fickle public sentiment, and criticism from practitioners and academics, large technology companies are taking steps toward defining what responsible AI use means today. As data scientist Tom Slee wrote, these companies at least recognize that "they must establish reputations as responsible stewards of these powerful technologies *if they are to avoid a costly backlash*" (emphasis added).[8]

Platform companies, social media businesses, and many more outside of the tech industry have already deployed AI that yielded negative consequences. Are post hoc concern and corrective action enough to meet the ethical bar?

New motivations will likely emerge over time. Regulations and laws will continue to emerge, compelling companies to comply with standards of responsible AI use. The general public, for its part, is becoming more aware of AI and its potential harms, and the trust consumers place in a company is likely to increasingly be shaped by trust in the AI tools it uses.

Alongside this, business policies and industry standards will be developed more broadly, the adherence to which could become a competitive advantage in the marketplace. After all, would you do business with a company that disregards questions of responsibility rather than another that does not?

Motivations notwithstanding, the overall lesson is that even as groundbreaking AI is created by some of the most brilliant people alive, we cannot assume their technical mastery means they are simultaneously ethical savants who can think through every potential outcome, good and bad. Going forward, all companies must contend with the reality that the "Wild West" days of AI are evolving into a more structured and inclusive system of processes and decision making that orbit the core question: Is using this AI the responsible thing to do?

Balancing Good, Better, and Best

Chief Operations Officer Elsa found the data science team as they returned from lunch and led them into the lab.

"Explain to me this concept around a 'customer personality assessment from Internet scrape,'" she said and pointed to the whiteboard.

One of the junior data scientists was eager to explain.

"We can definitely build this. It's part NLP, part sentiment analysis, really great stuff. The idea is we feed it names of our customers' employees, and it scrapes data from their social media use, notices in their local areas, and so forth. And *then* we expand to include all of *their* contacts, and the system can then tell our salespeople important insights to help the sale."

Elsa shook her head and said, "What kinds of insights?"

"Well, if a customer's friend just bought a new house and sentiment analysis tells us our customer is envious, we can help the sale by suggesting if they buy from us, it will be good for their employer, in turn good for him, and then he can afford that nice house."

"Do you realize how manipulative that is? Selling is not our only priority."

Unlike at BAM Inc., decisions on whether a given AI deployment is responsible are unlikely to be painted in black and white. Some use cases may be blatantly unethical and contrary to the social contract most enterprises aspire to uphold. But in many instances, uncertainty in responsible deployment may instead center on whether the tool has been sufficiently trained to avoid harm and provide benefit. If a model is only delivering 50% accuracy, is it responsible to deploy it? Well, it depends.

Take a tumor screening system that reviews MRIs and spots small growths on par with or even better than radiologists. However, while its detection rate is high, its false positive rate is also high. It is right 50% of the time. While that accuracy is quite low by data science standards, for the patient whose cancer is caught early, the AI tool is supremely valuable, even if it is wrong half the time. For the organization that developed such a tool, responsibility is a matter of application and potential value.

Likewise, facial recognition systems used by law enforcement can cut both ways in responsible use. If law enforcement uses facial recognition in a way that infringes on privacy and human rights, then the use is clearly irresponsible. However, if the same system is used to spot victims of human trafficking who can then be rescued, there is almost a moral obligation to use it. The axiom that warns that perfect should not be the enemy of good is apt for these ethical calculations.

It becomes clear as we break open the gray area of responsibility that the decisions rely not on a universal concept of right and wrong but on the local and regional societal mores, the needs of society and the marketplace, and the internal principles an enterprise has decided are important for their business culture and operations.

Thus, determining whether deploying an AI tool is a responsible choice is a whole-of-enterprise activity, involving all stakeholders from the executive suite to the most junior data scientist. It requires a diversity of perspectives and lived experiences. It also takes a cohesive enterprise strategy that percolates and informs department priorities. It demands a shared sense of accountability and an acknowledgment that when working with AI, there is a necessary standard of care. As well as considering whether they can create a novel AI solution, businesses must also weigh whether they should.

Put Your AI to the Test on Responsibility

- Is your organization using AI in a way that is responsible in terms of its impact on the business, the stakeholders, the end users, and the wider society and environment?
- Have you asked whether you should deploy a model given potential risks? Have you identified the risks? Who is involved in the decision about whether it is a responsible choice to use an AI, despite risks?
- Do you have a strategy for making decisions on responsible AI use? Does that strategy reflect the business culture and values? Was there a diversity of people and thought in the development of the strategy and values?
- Does the potential good that a model can achieve outweigh the potential negative outcomes it could cause? Has your organization asked, is this worth it?
- Are there laws or regulations governing how models can be used given concerns over environmental protection, social equity, data protection, and public safety and wellbeing?
- Are the stakeholders motivated to think about responsibility in their interaction with the model? How are they motivated? Are there channels for stakeholders to provide feedback and note concerns?

Leading Practices in the Responsible Use of AI

Ethics in business is a cross-cutting imperative that is technology agnostic. The common guidelines of CSR and a "doing well while doing good" mindset are appropriate, but in AI specifically, there are additional activities enterprises should explore when attempting to answer the complicated topic of responsible AI use. To aid discussions and deliberations, some of the leading practices that can support the responsible AI include:

Lead with Principled Strategy

Executives have a vital role in determining the business culture and the values of the enterprise. Determine the principles for how AI tools and their use cases are evaluated. This should go deeper than high-level sentiments. Rather, every stakeholder needs clear guidance on how decisions ought to be made when it comes to responsible AI use, as well as the other characteristics of trustworthy AI. In this way, the ethical priorities that are aligned with enterprise strategy in the boardroom can be carried throughout the organization and the myriad professionals involved in high-stakes AI decisions.

Charge an AI Advisory Board with Oversight

An AI Advisory Board can provide the right guidance on matters that might not rise to the level of executive concern but nevertheless require broader input than a single department. The board is charged with thinking through and weighing in on all the factors that touch trustworthy AI, including its responsible use. This can include things such as reviewing procurement decisions and exploring whether a vendor's model aligns with the established business principles. It might also include assessing whether a model's accuracy is sufficient for use and if any harms could arise because of it.

Intentionally Build Diversity

AI is shaped entirely by the people who build it and the data they select. The responsible application of AI demands a multitude of voices, perspectives, and lived experiences. We all have our own biases and limits to our knowledge. A diverse team is best positioned to think through all of the uses and misuses of an AI tool, helping to shape its function and purpose, as well as contributing to discussions over whether it can be responsibly used.

Define Processes for AI Assessments

Responsibility assessments should not be made at the end of the AI lifecycle. They should occur throughout it. At each stage, from ideation to real-world management, the enterprise should have established points where the project is reviewed, input is gathered, and decisions are made to shape the endeavor. One reason this is important is that once an AI is trained, it is challenging to un-train it. A better approach is to embed considerations of responsibility in the lifecycle itself.

Trust Emerging from Responsibility

For Elsa, the data scraping idea was an easy no. She and other executives had already discussed the ethical principles that guide AI application, and she knew where the red lines were. The fact that the data science team imagined such a tool was no slight against them. That's their job – to innovate and build things that deliver a competitive advantage. It was because she and others were engaged with the AI stakeholders that they were able to steer the data science efforts in other directions.

It was, she thought, the ideal scenario. Everyone had a role to play, and when the principles and the people aligned, it positioned the enterprise to make the right choices not after deployment but before the idea ever left the drawing board. It prevented potential harm, but it also saved effort, time, and money that could be put to more valuable and responsible applications.

When AI is deployed at scale, its implications are tremendous. Enterprises using these powerful tools wield huge influence and impact. It can be a force for good, bolstering the social contract with the public and inspiring ever greater levels of trust not just in AI but also in the business using it. But if slim attention is given to the potential harms and the all-important question of responsibility, the ramifications may only be known after the fact.

Every enterprise must determine independently what it deems to be right, assess the laws and regulations that might apply, and the social expectations of the people they serve. That can in turn inform just what constitutes the responsible use of AI.

Science is what we understand well enough

to explain to a computer. Art is everything

else we do.

– Donald Knuth

Chapter 11
Trustworthy AI in Practice

T o this point, we have investigated the qualities and nuances of the various dimensions of trustworthy AI. Armed with this insight and information, the next step is to convert knowledge into action. The discussions, strategies, and tactics for promoting trustworthy AI differ depending on the business, the function within the business, and the tool's use case. What is relevant to one may be unnecessary to another.

Recognizing that, the path forward is taking the insights from the dimensions of trust and using them as guidance for the steps the enterprise takes toward developing and deploying trustworthy AI. This is a tall order, in as much as standards, expectations, laws and regulations, and operating environments can differ between applications, business models, and geographies. Just because an AI tool is trustworthy in one instance does not mean that trust translates automatically to other use cases.

Nevertheless, despite the complexity, there are universal approaches and principles that can help an enterprise navigate this multifaceted landscape. The leading practices discussed in preceding chapters can lead organizations toward trustworthy AI, but they should be harmonized into a coherent and consistent regime that not just treats one model or use case but can govern the enterprise's entire AI strategy and operations. The methods for doing so can be grouped into three broad steps.

Step 1 – Identify the Relevant Dimensions of Trust

Each AI tool and use case should be considered on its own merits and application. Trustworthy AI does not mean every dimension of trust is satisfied. A predictive supply chain model that makes real-time recommendations for sourcing materials touches only certain dimensions of trust, such as reliability and transparency. If the tool makes inconsistent or erroneous predictions, that has a significant impact on the enterprise and trust in the tool itself. Fairness and safety, however, are unlikely to be relevant for trust in such a tool. For every organization, the task is to identify the operational scenarios where a dimension of trust may be relevant and then orient the entire AI lifecycle around tactics and decisions that satisfy the relevant trustworthy factors.

Yet, how do we determine which dimensions of trust are pertinent? Standardized checklists are unlikely to be sufficiently nuanced and flexible for making these decisions. Instead, the enterprise should look for input and concerns from its human capital – the enterprise leaders, business unit managers, and every employee who touches the AI lifecycle. Their varied perspectives, experiences, and job duties can together offer a rich source of insights that help decision makers determine the dimensions of trust that may be most relevant.

A COO, for example, may see no concern for privacy or security in a given tool, while the head of security may identify an issue others miss by virtue of her expertise in the subject matter. Likewise, an employee who grew up in an underserved community may identify problems with fairness and bias that go unnoticed by others. And it is not just about engaging the workforce. There is an imperative to solicit input from all stakeholders, including the board of directors, customers, industry thought leaders, and even the public. This kind of diverse input is what is needed to navigate the trustworthy landscape. Identifying the dimensions of trust is a group effort that should be conducted upfront and then periodically throughout the AI lifecycle.

Step 2 – Cultivating Trust Through People, Processes, and Technologies

With an awareness of which dimensions are relevant, the organization is ready to take action. Step 2 is to look across enterprise functions and resources and identify how they can be shaped or adjusted to advance trustworthy AI. The resulting considerations and actions can be grouped into the categories of people, processes, and technology.

People

A company's AI stakeholders are not just its data science experts. Arguably, it is the presumption that AI is the province of PhD holders that has been a limiting factor in drawing in the multitude of perspectives and ideas that can make trustworthy AI viable and real. Yet, while business unit leaders and regular staff have important roles to play, they need to understand why AI trust is important and how it is engendered in the company's AI endeavors. This takes education.

Once leadership has agreed on which principles of trustworthy AI are important, they should communicate this to the workforce. This means not just providing an explanation of why the dimensions of trust are relevant generally but also why they are relevant to the employee specifically. Employees should have the opportunity and the tools to richly understand which principles of trust are important, why they are important, and critically, how the employee fits into the enterprise-wide framework and efforts to develop and deploy AI that can be trusted. People across the enterprise need to grasp and embrace their role in the AI lifecycle.

One approach toward this end is to augment the existing ethics training that employees often complete as a component of their continuous learning. Other approaches might include education workshops and resources for expanding the employee's knowledge and upskilling their capacity to work toward trustworthy AI.

Yet, who champions and structures this education? More broadly, who within the enterprise owns the responsibility to foster ethics and trust in AI programs? The enterprise should determine the kinds of roles that can be created and staffed to lead AI ethics in the organization. There are many approaches, and which is most workable and valuable depends on the business and its AI goals. An enterprise may hire a Chief Trust Officer or Chief AI Officer who can inform and shape decisions at the executive level. It might hire an ethicist and determine where that role is best nested beneath the C-suite. Or a business could stand up an AI advisory committee that engages stakeholders, creates working groups, and oversees AI governance in line with enterprise strategy.

Ultimately, a company might decide that all or none of these approaches are appropriate for its AI programs. The key insight is that trustworthy AI hinges as much on human decision making as it does on the technology itself, and the organization should pursue a whole-of-enterprise engagement strategy across its human workforce. This might even extend beyond the business to its vendors and suppliers. When relevant third parties understand the principles of trust that the company follows, they can respect and adhere to the organization's AI goals.

Processes

Having established who is a stakeholder in AI development, deployment, and management, the enterprise needs to codify the approaches to trustworthy AI in enterprise process. Fostering ethical AI is not an ad hoc (or post hoc) endeavor. It should be baked into the business strategy and operations. This means establishing identifiable waypoints for assessment and review, as well as coordinating opportunities for input, setting responsibilities and expectations, and soliciting the right support and advisory services to supplement as needed.

As a foundational component, ensure that questions around AI trust and ethics are raised in every business process, whether it be procurement, AI design and development, or partnering with a vendor to market a product. Just as a company addresses business ethics and regulatory compliance as a part of business process, so too should the company embed considerations for trustworthy AI throughout enterprise functions.

Not every process requires treatment for AI trust, but only the business can determine which processes touch the AI lifecycle. As such, interrogate every process to determine its relevance to AI and identify opportunities to amend the process such that it bolsters the drive toward trustworthy AI. This takes controls and governance mechanisms that guide and inform how stakeholders create, use, and manage cognitive tools. The company needs policies for AI ethics, established practices for working with the models, and key performance indicators to measure ethical operation.

Meanwhile, because AI tools are so powerful, particularly at scale, risk is a factor that must be not just acknowledged but managed. The root of risk management is risk analysis, and in that, a company's risk assessment team has a role to play. They require knowledge of AI ethics, the functionality of a given tool, and expert input from practitioners across the business. This full situational awareness permits AI risk assessment as a component of enterprise risk management. AI is just another tool in the toolbox, and so its risk to the organization should be evaluated as a component of (and not distinct from) business operations.

One risk area is regulatory compliance, which is a significant challenge for AI application given that country-specific laws and regulations are emerging around the world. The regulatory requirements of one nation may differ from another, and it is the responsibility of the organization to ensure AI practices are in line with AI rules where the business operates. Thus, the company's legal and compliance experts are vital partners in AI risk assessment and ethical use. This may come in the form of business groups overseeing regulatory compliance, a risk assessment office, or the executive of government relations. Whoever is responsible for guiding the business to meeting legal and regulatory expectations, they should be a part of the AI lifecycle and their input required by virtue of process.

Not all regulations and leading practices have been devised yet. With so much in flux in the AI space, compliance can be a moving target. One of the most important ways to solve for ethics and trust is documentation. It is vital for improving internal operations, as well as evidencing to rulemakers that the enterprise aspires to ethical AI application. Documentation means recording the work that was done, the approvals that were a part of the process, and the sign-off of specific individuals who reviewed the tool and use case and their reasons for doing so.

Documentation also refers to recording job requirements and obligations as they relate to AI. Who are the engineers, strategists, and business leaders who played a part in the AI development? Did they adhere to business processes and make decisions in line with company ethics and strategy? Accountability is always a factor in AI, and documentation makes accountability possible.

Technology

While AI models lack anima, they are not neutral factors in AI ethics and trust. The data used to train the model, the model's function, and its operation after deployment all impact whether it is a tool deserving of trust. As a precursor to any AI project, ask first, can the technology be used without violating the established dimensions of trust? More fundamentally, just because something can be created, does that mean it should be?

Presuming that a given tool can be ethically created and used, the task becomes one of determining what aspects of the technology need to be treated such that the resulting model aligns with the applicable dimensions of trust. As data is the bedrock of AI, rigorously inspecting AI technology for trust and ethics requires a deep understanding of and trust in the data used to train the model.

The nature of the technology also impacts dimensions of trust such as transparency, explainability, and privacy. In some cases (although not all), the ability to understand how and why a model delivers the outputs it does is fundamental to trustworthy AI. Determining which models require this varies depending on use cases and enterprise priorities. The imperative is to know when the dimensions of trust overlap with technical function, and armed with that awareness, make design and deployment decisions that align with the priority principles of trust and ethics.

After the AI tool has been developed, ensure that processes are in place that set guardrails for ethical function, helping stakeholders monitor when a model operates in ways that violate the desired level of trust. While the market is still developing, there are a growing number of services and solutions that can be paired with an AI model to aid in post hoc monitoring. Analytics tools can be used to explore datasets for bias, audit AI outputs, and help explain how models calculated those outputs.

One outcome of this focus on trustworthy technology is that it demands participation from multiple stakeholders, all guided with processes and documented to a granular degree. When people, processes, and technologies are aligned in pursuit of ethical AI, the result is an organization whose AI tools are not just powerful and valuable. They are worthy of trust.

Guidelines for Action on Trustworthy AI

Modern society has systems in which our technology functions. There are rules, leading practices, regulations, and much more that surround the tools we use. For AI, this sociotechnical system is still nascent. From the regulations that mandate actions for the public interest to the consumer expectation for ethical and trustworthy application of technology, the arena in which AI functions is a work in progress. This is simultaneously challenging and an opportunity for leading enterprises using AI. While the ethical path ahead may be unclear and demanding, the organizations that forge a path and deploy trustworthy AI can seize a competitive advantage while shaping the very system surrounding these powerful tools.

Absent an established sociotechnical system, enterprises today must work with guiding principles and actions that can begin to shape the trajectory of AI to a trustworthy future. Three core areas suited for immediate attention are establishing principles, being mindful of diversity and sustainability, and upskilling the workforce.

Principles

Armed with consensus around which dimensions of trust are most pertinent, agree on a set of ethical principles and priorities that guide how you treat and weight those dimensions. There is a balance to be found between AI usefulness, accuracy, and trustworthiness. To what degree should a tool be transparent? How much transparency is enough? Is the model too brittle to scale? Can privacy concerns be mitigated or should the tool be retired?

These principles surround the technology and seep into the company culture. Every stakeholder should appreciate their place in the AI lifecycle and understand the trustworthy principles that guide their decision making. This can extend beyond the company walls, shaping interactions and contracts with third-party vendors, informing leading practices in an industry, and contributing to the larger evolution of the AI sociotechnical system.

Contributing Factors

Whether an organization has worked with AI for some time or is just getting started, two bedrock qualities of a successful AI program are diversity and sustainability. AI is a reflection of human society, and for cognitive tools to reach their greatest potential, they need to be shaped through an inclusive approach that brings together a variety of people to shape the AI lifecycle. Build diverse advisory committees, fill newly created roles with professionals from a range of backgrounds and heritage, and actively seek input with a bias toward inclusion. There are valuable contributions to be realized when diversity is a foundational basis for developing trustworthy AI.

Meanwhile, AI solutions should be not just scalable but sustainable. Enterprise leaders need to consider the longer-term impact of the models they deploy and how to balance AI function, value to the company, and the sustainability interests of the wider population. This means weighing the sizeable energy demands for model training, monitoring the real-world impact of a deployed tool, and designing with sustainability in mind.

Human Capital Development

AI will only become more powerful in the years to come, and the twenty-first-century workforce needs to be AI-ready. Holding an advanced degree is not a prerequisite for participating in the AI lifecycle. However, workers do need a measure of AI literacy. How can the principles of trustworthy AI be communicated to the labor force if they lack a basic understanding of AI and how it functions? The road to trustworthy AI will take a tailored reskilling of employees such that they have sufficient knowledge to participate in the enterprise's AI endeavors.

Taking the Next Steps

It may be simultaneously intimidating and exciting that every organization using AI is operating on an evolving landscape. Even with all the power and impact of current AI capabilities, we are still only at the beginning of a technological transformation that will reshape the world. Because these are the early days of AI used at scale, there is no prescription for how to guarantee trustworthiness in novel tools. In the face of innovation, every business must calculate for itself which dimensions of trust are important and how to empower people, amend processes, and develop technology.

Because we are working with broad guidelines to inform our decision making on AI, there is every opportunity for innovation in the tasks, roles, and enterprise strategies surrounding AI. The future sociotechnical system is being shaped by the organizations deploying these tools today. We have an opportunity and responsibility to shape that system and the tools in it into something we can trust.

Imagination is more important than

knowledge. Knowledge is limited.

Imagination encircles the world.

– Albert Einstein

Chapter 12
Looking Forward

The future with AI is dazzlingly bright. Of course, today we are wrestling with substantial challenges that force us to break new ground and innovate to bring AI to its greatest potential. There is cause for concern, but it is also an enormous opportunity. Those working with AI are shaping the future while also seizing gains and market leadership along the way. And there are an untold number of businesses that are just getting started with AI or forging a path to scale and reward.

We are right to be excited about the potential in AI. It is transforming the world. What a remarkable time to be engaged with emerging technology. Yet, we should temper our enthusiasm with an acknowledgment that there are several thorny issues and unanswered questions that need to be addressed in our pursuit of AI value. Some of them are purely technical but many deal with uniquely human values, expectations, and desires. And at their root are dimensions of trust.

There is vigorous debate over which qualities are most essential for ethical AI, with as much disagreement as agreement. Yet, ethics as a priority is perhaps too narrow. We do not just want AI that reflects human values. We seek tools that we can rely on.

Just as we are confident that our cars will stop when we press the brakes, we need the same level of confidence that AI does what we expect and in the way we desire. That takes trust, and it won't emerge on its own.

The challenge of course, as has been shown, is that there is not one way to engender trust in AI. There are numerous ways, some of which likely have not yet been devised by innovative minds. The qualities of trustworthiness that matter for one use case may be irrelevant for another. Only the organizations building and using these tools can determine the difference. There are no ironclad rules, but there are valuable guidelines.

The framework described throughout this book offers a roadmap for interrogating AI projects, identifying the relevant qualities of trust, and using that knowledge to amend and improve the entire AI lifecycle. All trustworthy AI shares some of these dimensions:

- Fair and impartial
- Robust and reliable
- Respectful of privacy
- Safe and secure
- Responsible and accountable
- Transparent and explainable

When organizations probe these concepts and determine which are important for their AI plans, they are prepared to look toward real AI governance that bakes trust in the lifecycle and AI function. This leads to new roles and responsibilities, employee training, AI-specific strategy and decision making, and new technology requirements. Governance comes about as the business is transformed to extract the most value from AI.

The happy consequence from this approach is that whatever laws and regulations emerge in the years to come, businesses that work toward building and using trusted, ethical tools will be prepared for the technology expectations set by public sector institutions. Government rulemaking can be difficult to anticipate, and there will be differences between nations in what they mandate. Regardless, businesses focusing on dimensions of trust today can create governance mechanisms that prepare them for the laws and regulations that eventually come to fruition.

The result of all this activity is trustworthy AI.

One of the most exciting aspects of AI is that the methods for developing it are becoming ever more sophisticated. In the years ahead, new approaches and types of models will emerge. Technologies will be invented to grant more computational power. We will see the world around us reshaped by a technology that stands alone in the history of human innovation.

Generations from now, students of history will look back on the early twenty-first century as a moment of transition, much the way we study the world before the invention of computers. When we are judged by history, will we be seen as responsible stewards who guided the development of AI to its most trustworthy potential? That is a question we are capable of answering with our actions and decisions. Nowhere is this responsibility greater than in the enterprises building or using AI today.

This might instill pause or concern but, instead, let's use that awareness of our responsibility to motivate our actions. Innovation always raises new problems to solve. Transformative technologies like AI result in dynamic changes to existing systems. This takes time and purposeful attention. Having explored the qualities of trust and how they impact AI use, you are empowered with the knowledge needed to make good decisions in your AI endeavors.

What is the outcome? You know the tools you use are aligned with the company values and the expectations of the marketplace. You document every step of the AI lifecycle and have set up the teams and governance mechanisms that allow you to truly control and shape AI to its most valuable and trusted potential. There are strategies and processes in place, and the workforce is AI-ready, equipped with the knowledge and confidence that comes from training and education. Adhering to rules and regulations is tractable. Return on investment is measurable.

All of this is within reach, so long as trust is the guiding light for our AI efforts.

Notes

Chapter 1

1. Marie Curie, Nobel Lecture, December 11, 1911, Nobel Prize Outreach AB 2021, https://www.nobelprize.org/prizes/chemistry/1911/marie-curie/lecture/.
2. David Schatsky, Craig Muraskin, and Ragu Gurumurthy, *Demystifying Artificial Intelligence* (Deloitte, November 4, 2014).
3. Quoc V. Le et al., "Building High-Level Features Using Large Scale Unsupervised Learning," *Proceedings of the 29th International Conference on Machine Learning* (2012).

Chapter 2

1. Edsger W. Dijkstra, "The Humble Programmer," *Communications of the ACM* 15 (1972): 859–866.
2. Elisa Jillson, *Aiming for Truth, Fairness, and Equity in Your Company's Use of AI* (Federal Trade Commission, April 19, 2021).

3. John Rawls, *A Theory of Justice*, 2nd ed. (Harvard University Press, 1999).

4. Jon Kleinberg et al., "Algorithmic Fairness," *Advances in Big Data Research in Economics, AEA Papers and Proceedings* 108 (2018): 22–27.

5. Julia Angwin et al., "Machine Bias," *ProPublica*, May 23, 2016.

6. Jason Okonofua and Jennifer Eberhardt, "Two Strikes: Race and the Disciplining of Young Students," *Psychological Science* 26, no. 5 (2015): 617–624.

7. Tony Sun et al., "Mitigating Gender Bias in National Language Processing: Literature Review," *Proceedings of the 57th Annual Meeting of the Association for Computational Linguistics* (2019): 1630–1640.

8. Will Douglas Heaven, "Predictive Policing Algorithms Are Racist. They Need to Be Dismantled," *MIT Technology Review*, July 17, 2020.

9. Jon Kleinberg, Sendhil Mullainathan, and Manish Raghavan, "Inherent Trade-offs in the Fair Determination of Risk Scores," *Proceedings of the 8th Conference on Innovations in Theoretical Computer Science* (2016) https://arxiv.org/abs/1609.05807.

10. Aaron Klein, "Reducing Bias in AI-based Financial Services," Brookings Institution, July 10, 2020.

Chapter 3

1. Steve Jobs, "Stanford Commencement Address," 2005, https://news.stanford.edu/2005/06/14/jobs-061505/.

2. "Healthcare's AI Future: A Conversation with Fei-Fei Li & Andrew Ng," Stanford HAI, April 29, 2021.

3. ISO, "Assessment of the Robustness of Neural Networks," ISO/IEC TR 24029-1:2021.

4. Ronan Hamon, Henrik Junklewitz, and Ignacio Sanchez, "Robustness and Explainability of Artificial Intelligence," *JRC Technical Report* (European Commission, 2020).

5. "Artificial Intelligence: An Accountability Framework for Federal Agencies and Other Entities," GAO, June 2021.

6. Tim G.J. Rudner and Helen Toner, "Key Concepts in AI Safety: Robustness and Adversarial Examples" (Center for Security and Emerging Technology, March 2021).

7. Defense Innovation Board, *AI Principles: Recommendations on the Ethical Use of Artificial Intelligence by the Department of Defense* (U.S. Department of Defense, 2019).

8. *Artificial Intelligence* (GAO, 2021).
9. Yili Hong, Jie Min, Caleb King, and William Meeker, "Reliability Analysis of Artificial Intelligence Systems Using Recurrent Events Data from Autonomous Vehicles" (2021), https://arxiv.org/abs/2102.01740.
10. Louis Bethune et al., "The Many Faces of 1-Lipschitz Neural Networks" (April 2021), https://arxiv.org/abs/2104.05097.

Chapter 4

1. Dorothy Stein, *Ada: A Life and a Legacy* (MIT Press, 1985), p. 128.
2. Nicholas Diakopoulos, "Accountability, Transparency, and Algorithms," in *The Oxford Handbook of Ethics of AI* (Oxford University Press, 2020), p. 198.
3. OECD, Recommendation of the Council on Artificial Intelligence, OECD/LEGAL/0449, 2019.
4. European Commission, "On Artificial Intelligence – A European Approach to Excellence and Trust," COM(2020) 65.
5. Heike Felzmann et al., "Towards Transparency by Design for Artificial Intelligence," *Science and Engineering Ethics* 26 (2020): 3333–3361.
6. High-Level Expert Group on AI, *Assessment List for Trustworthy AI (ALTAI)*, European Commission.
7. Ethan Bernstein, "The Transparency Trap," *Harvard Business Review*, October 2014.
8. Netherlands Action Plan for Open Government 2018–2020.
9. *Transparency and Responsibility in Artificial Intelligence: A Call for Explainable AI* (Deloitte, 2019).

Chapter 5

1. John McCarthy, "The Little Thoughts of Thinking Machines," *Psychology Today* 17 (1983): 46–49.
2. Christoph Molnar, "Interpretable Machine Learning: A Guide for Making Black Box Models Explainable," 2019, https://christophm.github.io/interpretable-ml-book/.
3. Broad Agency Announcement, "Explainable Artificial Intelligence (XAI)," August 10, 2016.

4. Bryce Goodman and Seth Flaxman, "European Union Regulations on Algorithmic Decision-making and a 'Right to Explanation,'" *2016 ICML Workshop on Human Interpretability in Machine Learning*, New York (2016).

5. Sandra Wachter, Brent Mittelstadt, and Luciano Floridi, "Why a Right to Explanation of Automated Decision-making Does not Exist in the General Data Protection Regulation," *International Data Privacy Law* 7, no. 2 (2017): 76.

6. Marco Tulio Ribeiro, Sameer Singh, and Carlos Guestrin, "'Why Should I Trust you?' Explaining the Predictions of Any Classifier" (August 2016), http://dx.doi.org/10.1145/2939672.2939778.

7. Upol Ehsan et al., "Expanding Explainability: Towards Social Transparency in AI Systems," *ACM CHI Conference on Human Factors in Computing Systems* (May 2021).

Chapter 6

1. Isaac Newton, *Philosophiæ Naturalis Principia Mathematica* (1687).

2. Zhanna Malekos Smith and Eugenia Lostri, *The Hidden Costs of Cybercrime* (McAfee, 2020).

3. "AI: Using Standards to Mitigate Risks," 2018 Public-Private Analytic Exchange Program.

4. Beena Ammanath, David Jarvis, and Susanne Hupfer, *Thriving in the Era of Pervasive AI: Deloitte's State of AI in the Enterprise*, 3rd ed. (Deloitte Consulting, 2020).

5. Marco Barreno, "Can Machine Learning Be Secure?" In *Proceedings of the ACM Symposium on Information, Computer, and Communication Security*, March 2006; *see also* Blaine Nelson et al., "Exploiting Machine Learning to Subvert Your Spam Filter," In *Proceedings of First USENIX Workshop on Large Scale Exploits and Emergent Threats*, April 2008.

6. John Beieler, "AI Assurance and AI Security: Definitions and Future Directions," Office of the Director National Intelligence, presented at the Computing Research Association, February 2, 2020.

7. National Academies of Sciences, Engineering, and Medicine, "Implications of Artificial Intelligence for Cybersecurity: Proceedings of a Workshop" (Washington, DC: The National Academies Press, 2019), ch. 5.

8. Kevin Eykholt et al., "Robust Physical-World Attacks on Deep Learning Visual Classification" (2018), doi: 10.1109/CVPR.2018.00175.

9. Matt Fredrikson, Somesh Jha, and Thomas Ristenpart, "Model Inversion Attacks that Exploit Confidence Information and Basic Countermeasures" (2015), https://doi.org/10.1145/2810103.2813677.

10. Elham Tabassi et al. *A Taxonomy and Terminology of Adversarial Machine Learning* (National Institute of Standards and Technology, 2019).

11. Andrew Marshall, Raul Rojas, Jay Stokes, and Donald Brinkman, *Securing the Future of Artificial Intelligence and Machine Learning at Microsoft* (Microsoft, 2018).

12. Beena Ammanath, Frank Farrall, and Nitin Mittal, "It's AI's Turn for the DevOps Treatment," *The Wall Street Journal*, March 1, 2021. *See also* "MLOps: Industrialized AI," *Tech Trends 2021* (Deloitte Insights).

13. Marshall et al., *Securing the Future of Artificial Intelligence and Machine Learning at Microsoft*.

14. Ibid.

Chapter 7

1. Margaret H. Hamilton, "Acceptance Speech by Ms Margaret H. Hamilton," Universitat Politècnica de Catalunya, BarcelonaTech. October 18, 2018, https://www.upc.edu/en/press-room/pdfs/acceptance-speech-by-margaret-h-hamilton.pdf.

2. Norbert Wiener, "Some Moral and Technical Consequences of Automation," *Science* 131, no. 3410 (1960): 1355–1358.

3. "Parents Upset After Stanford Shopping Center Security Robot Injures Child," *ABC7 News*, July 12, 2016.

4. Omri Gillath et al., "Attachment and Trust in Artificial Intelligence," *Computers in Human Behavior*, 115, February 2021.

5. Tim Nudd, "Tinder Users at SXSW Are Falling for This Woman, but She's Not What She Appears," *Adweek*, March 15, 2015.

6. "Who to Sue When a Robot Loses Your Fortune," *Bloomberg*, May 6, 2019.

7. Emma Strubell, Ananya Ganesh, and Andrew McCallum, "Energy and Policy Considerations for Deep Learning in NLP," *In the 57th Annual Meeting of the Association for Computational Linguistics*, July 2019.

8. Stuart Russell, comment in "The Myth of AI: A Conversation with Jaron Lanier," *Edge*, November 14, 2014.
9. Iason Gabriel and Vafa Ghazavi, "The Challenge of Value Alignment: From Fairer Algorithms to AI Safety," in *The Oxford Handbook of Digital Ethics* (Oxford University Press, 2020).
10. *Odds of Dying* (National Safety Council, 2019).
11. Bryant Walker Smith, "Ethics of Artificial Intelligence in Transport," in *The Oxford Handbook of Ethics of AI* (Oxford University Press, 2020).
12. Pedro A. Ortega, Vishal Maini, and the DeepMind safety team, *Building Safe Artificial Intelligence: Specification, Robustness, and Assurance* (DeepMind Safety Research, 2018).
13. Smith, "Ethics of Artificial Intelligence in Transport."
14. David Leslie, *Understanding Artificial Intelligence Ethics and Safety: A Guide for the Responsible Design and Implementation of AI Systems in the Public Sector* (The Alan Turing Institute, 2019).
15. Ibid.

Chapter 8

1. Dennis Gabor, *Inventing the Future* (Penguin Books, 1972).
2. Samuel Warren and Louis Brandeis, "The Right to Privacy," *Harvard Law Review* 4, no. 5 (1890): 193.
3. *Charles Katz v. United States*, 389 US 347, 88 S. Ct. 507, 19 L. Ed. 2d 576, 1967.
4. Herman Tavani and Hames Moor, "Privacy Protection, Control of Information and Privacy-Enhancing Technologies," *ACM SIGCAS Computers and Society*, 31, no. 1 (2001): 6.
5. Deirdre Mulligan, Colin Koopman, and Nick Doty (2016), "Privacy Is an Essentially Contested Concept: A Multi-dimensional Analytic for Mapping Privacy," *Philosophical Transactions of the Royal Society A*, 374(2083).
6. *Artificial Intelligence and Privacy – Issues and Challenges* (Office of the Victorian Information Commissioner, 2018).
7. Yves-Alexandre de Montjoye et al., "Solving Artificial Intelligence's Privacy Problem," *The Journal of Field Actions Science Reports* 17 (2017).

8. Md Atiqur Rahman et al., "Membership Inference Attack Against Differentially Private Deep Learning Model," *Transactions on Data Privacy* 11 (2018).

9. Cameron Kerry, *Protecting Privacy in an AI-Driven World* (Brookings Institution, 2020).

10. *California Consumer Privacy Act (CCPA) – A Quick Reference Guide to Assist in Preparing for the CCPA* (Deloitte, 2019).

11. Leinar Ramos and Jitendra Subramanyam, *Maverick Research: Forget About Your Real World Data – Synthetic Data Is the Future of AI* (Gartner, 2021).

Chapter 9

1. Mohammed ibn-Musa al-Khwarizmi, *The Compendious Book on Calculation by Completion and Balancing* (820 CE).

2. Joshua Kroll, "Accountability in Computer Systems," in *The Oxford Handbook of Ethics of AI* (Oxford University Press, 2020).

3. Virginia Dignum, "Responsibility and Artificial Intelligence," in *The Oxford Handbook of Ethics of AI* (Oxford University Press, 2020).

4. Jason Millar et al., "Accountability in AI: Promoting Greater Societal Trust," *Discussion Paper for Breakout Session, G7 Multistakeholder Conference on Artificial Intelligence.* December 6, 2018.

5. Kroll, "Accountability in Computer Systems."

6. John Villasenor, "Products Liability Law as a Way to Address AI Harms," *Brookings Institution Artificial Intelligence and Emerging Technology Initiative*, October 2019.

7. John Danaher, "Robots, Law and the Retribution Gap," *Ethics and Information Technology* 18 (2016): 299.

Chapter 10

1. Grace Hopper, "Commencement Speech at Trinity College," 1987, https://newsfeed.time.com/2013/12/09/google-doodle-honors-grace-hopper-early-computer-scientist/.

2. Howard Bowen, *Social Responsibilities of the Businessman* (University of Iowa Press, 2013).

3. Committee for Economic Development, *Social Responsibilities of Business Corporations* (June 1971).

4. Elena Chatzopoulou. "Millennials' Evaluation of Corporate Social Responsibility: The Wants and Needs of the Largest and Most Ethical Generation," *Journal of Consumer Behaviour*, 20, no. 3 (2021).

5. Emma Strubell, Ananya Ganesh, and Andrew McCallum, "Energy and Policy Considerations for Deep Learning in NLP," *In the 57th Annual Meeting of the Association for Computational Linguistics*, July 2019.

6. AI and Compute, *OpenAI*, May 2018.

7. Matteo Cinelli et al., "Echo Chambers on Social Media: A Comparative Analysis" (2020). DOI: https://arxiv.org/abs/2004.09603.

8. Tom Slee, "The Incompatible Incentives of Private-Sector AI," in *The Oxford Handbook of Ethics of AI* (Oxford University Press, 2019).

Chapter 11

1. Donald Knuth, "Forward," in *A=B* (1997), https://www2.math.upenn.edu/~wilf/AeqB.pdf.

Chapter 12

1. George Sylvester Viereck, "What Life Means to Einstein: An Interview by George Sylvester Viereck," *The Saturday Evening Post*, October 26, 1929.

Index

199